REDEEMING FEAR

REDEEMING FEAR

A CONSTRUCTIVE THEOLOGY
FOR LIVING INTO HOPE

JASON C. WHITEHEAD

Fortress Press
Minneapolis

REDEEMING FEAR

A Constructive Theology for Living into Hope

Cover image © iStockphoto.com / Eveline Kooijman

Cover design: Tory Herman

Library of Congress Cataloging-in-Publication Data is available

Print ISBN: 978-0-8006-9914-7

eBook ISBN: 978-1-4514-3858-1

The paper used in this publication meets the minimum requirements of American National Standard for Information Sciences — Permanence of Paper for Printed Library Materials, ANSI Z329.48-1984.

Manufactured in the U.S.A.

This book was produced using PressBooks.com, and PDF rendering was done by PrinceXML.

For Elizabeth, Caitlyn, and Caroline—all of whom increase the possibility and probability for hope in my life

CONTENTS

Acknowledgments

Many people helped usher this book from a simple idea to what you have before you. I am grateful to Larry Kent Graham and Carrie Doehring at Iliff School of Theology in Denver, Colorado, who helped shape the initial project that gave birth to this book; Ted Dougherty and Jamie Beachy read various parts of the book and provided helpful feedback and comments; numerous editors encouraged me, offering advice and questions along the way; and, my family and friends checked in from time to time and pushed me to keep going. I can only supply a simple thank you to this cloud of witnesses for their guidance, help, and encouragement.

Introduction

We are emotional creatures. Our memories, our beliefs, our imaginations are all impacted by the emotions we experience on a daily basis. Emotions shape and color our world in truly fantastic and meaningful ways. However, our theologies and ideas about humanity often lack careful attention to our embodied emotional experiences. Moreover, the way we approach particular sources of knowledge, like scripture, often leads us to denigrate certain emotional experiences, rather than incorporate them as part of a complex relational sense of humanity and our relationship to God.

What we are learning through social psychology, the neurosciences, and other disciplines challenges many of our preconceived notions about humanity. These alternative sources of knowledge add to our theological ideas about what it means to be human. They complicate our traditional theologies and beckon us into understanding humanity with new eyes. What these scientists and psychologists have to teach us can feel threatening to the common beliefs we have held. At the same time, there is something truly hopeful about what we are learning. Each of these disciplines gives us new ways of understanding individual and group behavior. They help us understand how our communities of faith act and react to the world. They give us new ways of talking about human beings and reclaiming much of our embodied existence. This is a time for great ferment for theologians and people of faith, if we can be open to incorporating some of this new knowledge into our theological lives together.

Fear, in particular, is one of the emotional whipping posts of theologians and pastors. Sermons and books on fear often claim that the Bible is clear that fear is detrimental to humanity. Frequently, the thrust of these traditional arguments is that fear is never your friend, never your ally. Like many strong emotional states (anger, ecstasy, grief, etc.), fear is a suspicious state of being. Moreover, since it often co-opts our more rational ways of interpreting the world, it is often seen as dangerous to a well-thought-out faith; or alternatively, it is thought of as revealing a weakness of faith or a dependency on God.

What we fail to see is that fear can be an ally; it is the emotion that ensures our survival in the face of traumatic experiences or threats to our being. Fear is the emotion that helps us navigate a sometimes hostile and often unpredictable world. However, the ways that we—evangelical and mainline theologians—talk about fear lack the appropriate complexity to understand its

1

theological importance for our lives. My work here is to help you understand the positive and adaptive qualities of fear. Most importantly, it is to help you see how God remains present in those moments of fear, calling us into a greater life and greater awareness of the possibilities of hope in this world.

This is a book about God and the emotions of fear and hope. It is about the stories we create and tell concerning the world and our experiences of it. Some of this material is personally and theologically challenging. It describes a novel way of theologically experiencing the world, as well as how that new view impacts our relationships with communities, people, and objects all around us. As this book progresses, I will help you understand fear from theological, neurological, sociological, evolutionary, and psychological perspectives. Taken together, these disciplines provide a complex picture of the emotion of fear and its relationship to hope.

This is a theological text, written by a Christian practical theologian. My approach is to create a collaborative conversation between a number of disciplines in order to tease out a complete picture of fear. I believe theology needs to critically engage a variety of disciplines in a way that challenges the presuppositions of each discipline. For example, neurophysiological data help us understand the brain and body's reaction to fear; sociological data help us see how fear impacts relationships, society, and community; psychological data help us grasp the ways fears are constructed in our memories and how that impacts our beliefs; evolutionary data help us understand the conservation and importance of specific areas of the brain and their associated behaviors; finally, theology helps us put all of these disciplines together in ways that discern the impact and meaning of fear. This allows us to explore our relationship with a God who obviously sees a need for us to be afraid at certain points in our lives. The value of this approach is that each discipline teaches us something about what it means to be afraid, making fear more complex and helping us understand it better.

Over the course of this book, this complex view of fear—an embodied emotion we all experience—will challenge many of our traditionally held beliefs about emotions. Fear most often arises in situations of threat or trauma. When we experience a threat, whether firsthand or vicariously, our memories encode specific emotions onto the stories we tell about that moment in time. Fear can sweep through communities and impact the way we relate to one another. It can form and shape a worldview that causes us to retreat from things we perceive as hostile. However, it can also be a great source of hope. Reflecting on the times we are afraid can also reveal some of the things we hope for most.

I imagine one initial reaction might be, "Wait, I haven't been threatened or traumatized." You might also think, "Hey, the Bible tells me over and over again to not be afraid." Those are certainly valid reactions to reading these first few paragraphs. Furthermore, based on your experiences and the sources you use to define your faith, it may be hard to create the space needed to reframe and redeem what it means to be afraid. Yet, it is my hope that you will try. The emotion of fear is a vital and inescapable part of human life. If we can find ways to understand this emotional state, using all of the tools at our disposal, then we may come to see the life-giving qualities of fear. In addition, we can be more intentional about the hopes that run underneath and parallel with our experiences of fear.

Neuropsychologist Joseph LeDoux says that the emotion of fear is conserved "to a large extent across human cultures."[1] This means that we all possess a neuropsychological capability for experiencing the emotion of fear. For me, our journey begins with this simple statement—one that reveals an innate physiological ability to feel the emotion of fear. However, to lean our entire understanding of fear on our physiology would be remiss. We are meaning-making creatures, and understanding fear as inescapable deserves some interpretation, especially from theological circles. Therefore, while our first steps on this journey are to understand our capacity for fear, our final steps will allow us to see the implicit hopes we carry with us at all times; and, by the last page I think you will discover how the hopes of our lives, born in the stories we tell, are especially present in our experiences of fear.

The Impact of Fear

Imagine sitting in your office when Sandra walks through the door. She seems tired, and a bit forlorn. She sits, actually collapses may be a better way of describing it, into the chair across from your desk. With great effort she tells you of being mugged outside of her apartment while walking home from work. She tells you how she cannot be out after dark; how she is afraid of every shadow; how she no longer goes out with friends and has moved into the safe basement of her parents' house. Sandra tells you that she jumps every time a man appears at her office door at work. She is exhausted from always being "on" or "aware." She wonders where God was, why this happened to her, and what to do with this fear she constantly lives with now.

You meet Jim for coffee one day. A longtime friend, something has changed recently with him. He seems more angry and bitter about the world. He wears his hostility to anything different on his sleeve. You listen as he disparages others who don't believe the same thing he does. He spits out the names of politicians and terrorists. You are surprised to hear that he has purchased several guns, and that he is stockpiling food and survival gear. Jim has cut off a lot of the relationships that were previously meaningful to him, preferring to live in an isolated rather than interactive world.

Calvary Church, the community of faith you were called to help, seems resigned to its fate. Made up of mostly older members, half of them seem despondent at their chances of survival. The other half are afraid that what they worked so hard to build will die with them. The mixture of resignation and bitterness runs deep in the story of the community. They worry that changing things will dissolve the bonds of their community, but the alternative of a slow death is equally dissatisfying. So they are resolute in their choice to do nothing. Their fear paralyzes them and they turn their focus to a world that they believe misunderstands them and attacks their community. With little hope, they meet week after week, to worship, to bury their dead, and to insulate themselves from the changes that go on around them.

In each of our lives, fear will impact the ways we relate to one another and to the world around us. Seemingly random events will be interpreted as traumatic. Communities will develop stories of feeling threatened by the outside world or even their own finitude. Events like these shape our worldview, our faith, and our ability to imagine hopeful futures. I am not under the impression that everyone has experienced something so traumatic firsthand. However, we all experience tragedy and trauma on a daily basis.

In the past, when a significant tragedy occurred, its greatest impact was on those who witnessed it. To be sure, information got around, but it took days or months. The comfort of being removed from tragedies changed with the onset of radio and television. We no longer had to wait to know what was happening in and around the country and the world. As technology improved, twenty-four-hour news channels and instantaneous reporting on the Internet proliferated, bringing tragedies to our living rooms as they unfold. Rather than having to seek out information on tragic events, today we have to seek out places where the tragedies cannot find us.

Sandra's story encapsulates some of our reactions to tragic and traumatic events. She runs from the world and significant relationships, fearing another trauma. As we continue to bear witness to events like 9/11, the unfolding economic breakdown, natural disasters, war, riots, crime, and terrorism, a basic level of fear permeates the culture and our relationships. Jim's anger and bitterness, his insistence on survival and fighting the world, is a natural reaction to an overwhelming fear. He begins to live suspiciously, wary that someone or something is out to get him. For Calvary Church, the fear has permeated the community and a mixture of resignation and suspicion governs their life together. In all of these cases, fear has taken root and we have little to no theology that understands the complexities of the emotion of fear, and how we might continue to live faithfully with hope in a sometimes hostile and unpredictable world.

A Remedy in Process

Providing a remedy for Sandra's experiences following her mugging could take shape in a number of ways. Most often, people of faith have looked to scripture to provide the antidote to our fear-based narratives. We might scan a concordance and seek out some of the four hundred plus verses where the word *fear* is used in the Bible. In doing so, we might become a little confused. There are several ways to think about fear. Certainly, the human experience of fear is well represented throughout the Bible, confirming that fear is an oft-experienced emotion. In other places, the word *fear* expresses the feeling of awe that one has when approaching God. While adding some complexity, this interpretation is of little use to those who have encountered threatening images, people, ideas, or events. It might even serve to remind us how awesome or terrible the power of God can be, turning God into a deity that we wouldn't want to come and lay our burdens before. In the end though, most people focus on the passages that admonish us not to have fear. They might close in on Jesus' words in the Gospels that exhort us to take risks for faith; words that remind us that God is with us when we confess our faith and live boldly, even at the risk of alienation from those who do not understand the faith in God that strengthens our resolve. The ramifications of these words are many, and admonishments such as these, repeated by human mouths, can affect us in myriad ways. Depending on the tone used to express the sentiment, I can imagine the reaction of a fearful person running the gamut from relief to shame. That presents a problem when talking about the emotion of fear.

A strictly biblical approach can oversimplify the importance of the emotion of fear to human survival and coping, as well as its essential embodiment in our created selves. Furthermore, it is important to remember that throughout the biblical text when we are told not to have fear, we are also given a reason for the truth of this claim. In most instances where the phrase "do not fear" is used, it is accompanied by God's response "for I am with you." We cannot underestimate the importance and power these words of comfort might hold as we continue to work with our fear-based stories. God's immanence is a vital part of any theological interpretation of the emotion of fear. Moreover, remembering that

God is with us can provide a powerful metaphor for the stories of threat and trauma that we create and share with the world. The biblical account of God's co-creative presence in the world provides an important starting point for understanding the need to explore fear faithfully. At the same time, we cannot ignore the large body of research in the world that helps us further understand what happens when individuals and cultures live through a worldview of fear.

To be a human being is to experience the world through multiple lenses, including our faiths, emotions, thoughts, and senses. The emotion of fear is an integral part of these experiences and vital to the ways we adapt to the world meaningfully. To really understand the emotion of fear, what it means to be afraid, we must engage the different sources of knowledge that seek to understand this important emotional state. This is not learning for learning's sake. I want you to see this as an opportunity to live into our God-gifted emotional capacities.

Furthermore, this is a chance to explore the idea that we cannot be afraid without also being hopeful that something in our lives is worth living for. Fear does not just protect us *from* a threat or trauma; it protects us *for* something as well. You will not find any admonitions on my part to be fearless; I think, even with the best of intentions, that is a naïve position to take. Instead, you will find me taking an integrative approach to understanding fear. My approach to the emotion of fear takes the evidence from multiple sources of knowledge seriously. I use this information to construct meaningful theological statements about fear and hope, which then guide the practices examined at the end of this book.

REDEEMING FEAR, PIECE BY PIECE

This book is divided into four parts, with each part introducing a new aspect of fear and/or its redemption. Taken as a whole, the book creates an argument for a particular understanding of the emotion of fear and how it relates to hope. The first part examines the difference between fear and anxiety, as well as the sociological evidence for a "Culture of Fear." In the first chapter, I explore two things. The first is a general examination of emotions, theology, and God. The second deals with the ways we define fear and anxiety, teasing out how they differ from one another. In order to build a meaningful framework to understand fear, we must be able to recognize its specific hallmarks apart from other emotions. This chapter provides an early framework and definition of fear that guides the remainder of the book. This enables us later to understand how fear and hope are intertwined with one another.

In the second chapter, I introduce some research from sociologists around the world. Through their research and theories, we begin to see how a culture or fear permeates the social fabric in the United States. So often, we live and move through our worlds uncritically. We sometimes find ourselves tacitly accepting the messages we are handed and the accompanying emotions the narratives engender. The constant bombardment of political, religious, and social messages can feed our innate ability to experience the emotion of fear. The rise of the emotion of fear elicits particular actions and reactions to the world in which we live and move and have our being.

The second part of this book is concerned with the embodied genesis of the emotion of fear and how that impacts the ways we relate to the world and one another. In chapter three, I share one of my own fears and how we might understand the embodied and embedded reaction I have to spiders. This chapter looks at the neurophysiological characteristics of fear, the conservation of fear in our evolutionary history, and how our memories are affected by the emotion of fear. The importance of this research cannot be understated. If we are truly going to understand our capacity to experience the emotion of fear and how it is an essential part of our createdness, then we need to have a rudimentary understanding of how our brain is wired to feel fear.

Chapter four takes shape around the notion that the emotion of fear can be shared in communities and relationships. This chapter explores how fear is transmitted socially by looking at several illustrations as well as asking you to draw from your own experiences. From these brief illustrations, we will move into a more in-depth look at Calvary Church and examine how fear-based narratives can permeate the stories of communities. When coupled with the emotion of fear, the stories we tell are lived out through the ways we behave around one another. After a brief analysis of the case, we will turn to a broader theological examination of fear.

The third part of this book begins to make a theological turn in interpreting the emotion of fear and its relationship to hope. While I believe that a theology of fear is present throughout this book, this third section makes an explicit turn to developing a theological understanding of the emotion of fear. In the two chapters in the section, I work with process theology to achieve a number of goals to help you understand fear and hope as intertwined with one another.

Chapter five introduces process theology as the primary theological interpretive lens for this project. I introduce a process view of God's relational power and presence with the world. Then, utilizing a process-relational framework, I create an understanding of fear as a faith-filled emotional response to particular experiences. If we truly understand ourselves as creative co-creators of reality, then it is important that we begin to think of fear as something that is adaptive to the world live in, as well as revealing of our relationship with God.

Chapter six explores the relationship between fear and hope. It begins by examining what it means to have hope. By exploring psychological and theological ideas, we come to see that hope is about possibilities and probabilities. This includes taking a look at how fear and hope are intertwined in experiences, as well as how hope provides clues that can mitigate the impact of fear-based stories. In this chapter, resistance and resilience are introduced as primary themes related to the ways human beings experience hope in the midst of threats and trauma.

The final section of this book explores the power individuals have in shaping and creating stories of hope from those that originated out of fear. In the seventh chapter I explore some ideas about reframing and retelling our fear-based stories. Part of overcoming the fears we carry with us is not found in denying them. It is not about repressing the stories that haunt us or believing we are to go through life fearless. Fear is an essential part of our createdness and an inescapable part of our emotional lives. So is hope. As we make meaning and sense of the stories we tell, often the best we can do is to understand our reaction of fear and not be ashamed of feeling it. Furthermore, in moments of reflection when we tell our stories again, we can begin to shine light into the cracks of these narratives. Within each story of fear there are multiple accounts of the ways in which we resist these narratives. These small hopes can be made to shine upon that which threatens us, lessening the impact of fear and placing it within the context of its intended use.

The eighth chapter develops some theological ideas concerning the use of fear in the public sphere. The cultural exploitation of fear by political and religious figures has created a relational divide that exacerbates issues and disrupts our ability to communicate effectively with one another. Looking at the reporting of crime, I explore the need for a more robust relational emphasis. Then, using the process notions of beauty, creativity, novelty, and harmony, I explore how the abuse of fear narrows our choices and isolates us from others. A public theological response to the stories of fear dumped into the cultural milieu centers on creating stories of contrast that protest the manipulations we experience. In conjunction with the call to live out the love ethic, I introduce the prophet Micah's call to kindness, humility, and justice as the acts of faith that can drive out these narratives that call us to live in fear.

In the ninth chapter, I explore what it means to be kind, humble, and just. These three acts of faith provide the kind of response that can transform stories of fear. Together they protest these stories and provide alternative narratives that speak more to the love we are called to exhibit. Moreover, they provide specific actions we can take that create novel stories of hope that can bring us into greater community. Thus we have the power to find beauty not just in the contrast between these stories, but the capability of creating a more intense harmony that reveals God's intent of an ever-increasing sense of beauty in our lives. At the end of this chapter, we will return to Calvary Church and explore some novel possibilities based on these ideas.

The conclusion of this book seeks to draw together everything we have discussed along the way. As a concluding statement, it provides a final argument for ideas presented throughout the course of the book. Ultimately, I leave it to you to decide if the emotion of fear and what it means to be afraid has been transformed and/or redeemed. All I ask is that you keep an open mind throughout your reading. Take each chapter as it comes and seek to integrate it with how you understand God and faith. Where do you feel comforted? Where do you feel challenged? What questions does an argument call up for you? Which ideas help you see God or your practices of faith through new eyes?

The movement of this book is from explanation to action, from theory to practice. Any text that purports to explain our relationship to the emotion of fear without fully exploring its sociological, evolutionary, and especially its physiological roots, only tells part of the story. Likewise, any text that only sees fear through these same physiological roots without acknowledging the role that interpretation and meaning-making play in our lives is remiss as well. We must begin to acknowledge that fear, indeed all emotions, are a part of a complex interpretive web that helps us understand the world. Emotions drive our passions and remind us of the beauty of the world around us. The emotion of fear is nothing to fear; and, we should not be shamed into thinking that because we experience fear we are weak. Without fear we lose access to part of what gives us a passion for life, and in losing that, we lose the need for hope.

Notes

1. Joseph E. LeDoux, "Emotion: Cues from the Brain," in *Foundations in Social Neuroscience*, ed. J. T. Cacioppo et al. (Cambridge, MA: MIT Press, 2002), 389.

PART 1

Why Fear? Why Now?

In part 1, I want you to think about the question "why" or "why now?" The chapters in this section examine the need for exploring the emotion of fear through our current cultural milieu. In chapter 1, I open by exploring the need for conversation between literature on emotions and theology. This exploration takes us into the long held doctrine of the impassability of God. In addition, I explore the differences between anxiety and fear, as well as how they have been conflated in our common cultural language.

In chapter 2, I look at how threats are generated in our current culture. By exploring the ways in which we consume media stories about terrorism, crime, and humanity, I put forth the idea that we are living in a culture of fear. This is an unprecedented time when humanity has access to global events at their fingertips. Thus, this is also a time in history when the threats of the world are commonly known and digested by anyone with access to the news, newspaper, or an RSS news feed.

Throughout this part of the book, I build the case that a new examination of fear is warranted; it is a "why now" set of propositions meant to help us see the necessity of exploring fear in new and complex ways. As you go through these first two chapters, I will refer back to the case examples mentioned in the introduction. It will be helpful if you keep these three diverse examples in mind as we move through the chapters, as they will help ground your reading of this text.

1

This Emotional Life

God was angry and . . .
They changed their ways and God had
compassion . . .
Jesus went into the temple and turned over
the tables of the money changers . . .
Jesus wept . . .

The Bible is full of moments when God and Jesus act with a passion driven by their emotions. Anger, compassion, love, sadness, and even fear all have places in the biblical narrative. God is often described as angry, jealous, compassionate, and/or loving. Yet, over time, Christian doctrine has been shaped by God's omnipotence and omniscience ("all-powerful-ness" and "all-knowing-ness") rather than God's empathic abilities. In fact, we even have a longstanding historical doctrine (called the impassability of God) that describes God's lack of true emotional experience. As we absorb these views of God, we come to the conclusion that to be more like God is to be a well-reasoned and impassioned actor in the world. In turn, our faith and concepts of God suffer from a lack of emotional and impassioned experience. Nowhere is this truer than in the mainline church of which I am a part. We pride ourselves on our thinking faith—on our ability to reason, reflect, and weave together science, rationality, and faith. It's not that we eschew emotions; they just occupy a space in the backgrounds our faith. There is nothing wrong with a well-reasoned faith; yet, there may be something wrong with a faith that does not open itself to the impact and possibilities that emotions provide. Emotions should be vital parts of our faith and life; they are the components of experience that make life more than just a series of facts; emotions make our dreams and imaginings possible and worthy of pursuit. Therefore, we do ourselves a disservice when we discount or vilify any emotional experience, whether it is anger, fear, joy, or sadness.

Our Emotional Life

Emotions are embodied aspects of our brain that enable us to cope with complex experiences quickly and actively. Let's break that down a bit. Emotions are embodied. They are a part of our brain's wisdom, and they are inescapable and adaptive. Neuropsychologist Joseph LeDoux (who has spent much of his career studying the emotion of fear) says that the word *emotion* is little more than "a label, a convenient way of talking about aspects of the brain and mind."[1] Like our higher cognitive functions (thinking, reflecting, interpreting, language, and so on), emotions are another system within the brain and mind that help us process the world in which we live, move, and become. LeDoux goes on to say that "[m]any emotions are products of evolutionary wisdom, which probably has more intelligence than all human minds together."[2] This is an interesting statement in that it not only puts the status of emotions on par with reason, but almost elevates the meaning and purpose of emotions to an uncontainable wisdom beyond that of simple reason.

We are emotional creatures; we are thinking creatures; we are expressive, active, reflective, embodied creatures. We are inescapably all of these things, as they are a part of our physical presence in the world. It is the connection between the embedded emotional systems of the brain and our ideas about our createdness that lead me to believe that all emotions are more vital to our lives, faiths, and experiences than we sometimes give them credit. Love, sadness, anger, and even fear are emotions that we often express uniquely based on our experiences. At the same time, it is widely thought that all human beings experience certain kinds of emotions regardless of culture, race, or gender. This conservation of certain emotions across wide landscapes of humanity should give us ample pause to reflect on the messages that a Christian faith shares about emotions in general. More specifically, it should give us a reason to engage the divine-human relationship around the topic of emotions.

Thus emotions must carry weight within the boundaries of our faith and life because they are meaningful parts of the *Imago Dei*.[3] The *Imago Dei* refers to the Christian way of talking about our intimate ties to the Creator. I use the term here to describe how we act as co-creators in the world, experiencing and interpreting it with God's help. When I consider humanity as made "in the image of God," it calls to mind both the certainty of a relationship to the divine, but also the possibilities created through our dynamic experiences of the world.

For me, the *Imago Dei* takes on figurative qualities as we are called to embody in our experiences who we understand God to be and how we believe God acts in compassionate and meaningful ways in the world. For this reason, our images of God should reflect our understanding of humanity, but also incorporate the idea that God is much more than we are, or can comprehend about ourselves.

FROM IMPASSABILITY TO EMPATH-ABILITY

The Impassability of God is a doctrine that originated with the early church as it sought to find its way and place in the pantheon of religions of that day. Impassability has its roots in Greek philosophy. It basically means "that God does not feel and/or experience emotions; God is, as Aristotle said three centuries before the church began, the unmoved mover."[4] As you can see, the doctrine we have inherited and debated throughout the years doesn't actually have its roots in Christian thought, but more so in the thoughts of Christians influenced by Greek philosophy.

Creating a vision of God as the unmoved mover, while attempting to preserve a laundry list of God's perfect qualities, ignores the passion and emotionality of the God we come to know in scripture. The simple truth is that they didn't have functional Magnetic Resonance Images of the brain as it lights up when we experience an emotion. Therefore, the way those early philosophers experienced emotions was as outside forces that derail us from the rational thoughts we are intended to have. As we have come to challenge conventional and historical thought about human beings, our theology and some of the doctrines we use to describe the divine-human relationship will continue to be challenged by the introduction of new knowledge. As we do this with emotions in particular, I am reminded of this statement: "Theological anthropology is enriched by affirming the essential and embodied nature of human emotions; they are one of God's greatest gifts to humankind."[5] Theological anthropology has to do with the impressions of humanity we hold to be true through the lens of faith. It is the merger of our sense of history, experience, reason, psychology, sociology, and theology into a picture that completes the sentence, "Human beings are . . ." Thus if we say "human beings are broken," we make a theological statement about sin, redemption, God's presence or absence, God's role as healer, guide, and sustainer. Our theological anthropology guides the kind of spiritual care we offer others; it impacts the ways we preach, teach, and lead communities of faith.

Think about the prophets, the early stories about God in scripture—even the life of Jesus reveals an emotional core. Take time to explore God's anger and frustration with humanity, which often permeates the texts we read. Go back and discover God's gentleness and compassion as they are woven throughout the stories of God's relationship with humanity. Turn to the Gospels and see the emotional life of Jesus play out in his ministry. The sorrow, love, anger, exhaustion, fear, and hope expressed throughout his meandering ministry saturate Jesus' interactions with people everywhere. There is simply little defense for the impassability of God, save for a human theologian's need for God to be perfect on all fronts. Even then, some form of perfect emotionality should be derived from the texts we call authoritative.

The difficulty we face with deconstructing a doctrine or a theology is twofold. First, how do we break with centuries of routine thinking? Second, how do we create what takes its place? To the first question, I can only propose that you allow yourself to be creative for a moment. Instead of thinking that God wants us merely to think clearly, what if we embrace the idea that God wants us to experience fully? What if we not only attempted to experience fully, but also believed that God experienced our lives fully as well? How would that challenge the conventional notions of God's relationship with us? To challenge long-held routine knowledge about God is to take a leap of faith. It means using the creative and imaginative gifts we have been given to see God in the ordinary and beyond. If a doctrine is going to hold up, we must be willing to challenge it, to challenge the routines of faith that we have been handed, and see in the end if the God we come to know is still worthy of worship.

To understand how we might replace the doctrine of impassability, I propose that we begin to think about God's empath–ability. You have already seen some of the support for this idea in paragraphs above that discuss God's emotional life in relationship with humanity. Through these words, we see that the impassability of God is a problematic doctrine to say the least. Furthermore, when we add these paraphrased words from scripture, "and God heard their cries,"[6] we can begin to envision anew the relationship between God and the emotions that shape the divine-human relationship.

To see God as "empathically-able" we must understand the meaning of empathy. Simply put, empathy is the ability to put yourself in another's shoes and "get" what they are feeling or experiencing. A colleague and mentor, Carrie Doehring, states that empathy is "making a connection with another person by experiencing what it is like to be that person, and . . . maintaining separation from the other person by being aware of one's own feelings and thoughts."[7] I think we can certainly make the case that God "gets" humanity; the leap we have to make is whether or not part of this connection to human beings is emotional as well. Insight is the ability to understand what someone else is thinking; this is different from empathy, which has a distinctly emotional flavor. To say that God is empathic is to believe in God's ability to experience the suffering, joy, pain, anger, hurt, fear, happiness that humans experience on a daily basis. It is to call God intimately immanent, yet at the same time that immanence is shared throughout all of humanity and the world.

While scripture and experience tell us a good deal about the empath-ability of God, process theology takes it one step further. Pastoral theologian Robert Thompson remarks that

> [w]ritings in process theology include some scant but clear statements about the suffering of God, which I think are significant for our exploration of emotions. If God suffers, and particularly if God suffers on account of the world, then we humans are reassured of God's care, which provokes feelings of assurance. Furthermore, as creatures made in God's image (a classical theological concept that I find meaningful), humans can also be reassured that, as God suffers, suffering will sometimes be our experience, and we can manage it with God's ever-present offerings of help. On the last page of his long and complex introductory book on process thought, Whitehead writes, "God is the great companion—the fellow-sufferer who understands" (Whitehead, 1978, p. 351).[8]

I think this view of God is refreshing. Not only does God experience the suffering we experience, but God, through this experience, also continues to offer us help by being present in a co-determinative relationship. To see God through the lens of empath-ability is to truly experience God as with us. To know that God takes in and empathizes with our experiences is to see God as a meaningful presence in our journeys of life and faith. It is to experience God as truly caring for us before, during, and after each moment that shapes our lives.

Empathy requires us to access and reflect upon the emotional content of our lives. It requires us to look beyond the facts, reason, or logic, and see the complexity of experiences as through a variety of lenses. Seeing God as empathic is vital to a meaningful faith. To believe that God truly cares, and doesn't just fake emotionality for our benefit, is less about making God in our image and more realizing that God's comprehension of the human condition is far beyond what we can explain. Furthermore, when we are empathic, having access to a myriad of emotions, we may be more fully bearing the image of God into the world.

Given what we know about the embodied nature of emotions, the doctrine concerning the impassability of God holds little truth for contemporary theology. Instead, I propose that we begin to shape our thoughts about God around the idea of empath-ability. By doing this, we can begin exploring emotions through a theological lens that values their impact. As a result, we can live into a faith that is more authentic to our experience of the world, as well as our experience of what it means to be made in the image of God. Simply put, we are empathic and emotional creatures; we are created in the image of God; therefore, God must have some experience of emotions, as well as the ability to empathize. While the logic may be as simple as 1 + 1 = 2, we must also be able to think broadly about the implications of this kind of concept of God.[9] This includes beginning to understand what we say when we claim to be afraid.

Fear and Anxiety

To say that God is empathic means that a wide variety of emotions are a part of the divine-human relational matrix. It means that in ways beyond our full comprehension, God suffers with us, loves with us, grows angry and indignant, and even understands and knows what it is like to experience fear. These are bold claims that are thrown in the direction of a mysterious God.[10] Humanity has often looked upon our emotions as weaknesses; my question to you is simply, what if they were all meant to be strengths? What if our embodied emotional experiences were meant to help draw us closer in our relationship with the divine? In the midst of that conversation, we must come to realize that *all* emotions must be a part of this relationship. We cannot simply separate good and bad, or positive and negative, and then attribute one set to God and another to humanity. Assuming we accept the argument that emotions are vital to the divine human relationship and, furthermore, that God shares in our experiences of emotional moments, then it is helpful to begin to construct ideas about these embodied emotions that speak to their adaptability, and their role in surviving, coping, and thriving in this world.

We can begin with understanding that there are some similarities shared by human beings. There are core emotional experiences that most, if not all, of humanity (and some of the animal kingdom) share. These core embodied emotions often include such things as anger, fear, happiness, sadness, and disgust. If we were to describe an emotional *Imago Dei*, these might be the places where we start to understand our embodied selves. Moreover, understanding emotions means realizing their uniqueness, and the ways they impact us on individual and relational levels. As we will see in coming chapters, fear is an adaptable emotion that orients us toward survival, coping, and thriving in the world. It is also one of the emotions, left to its own devices, that can drive us to separate ourselves from meaningful communities and relationships. Before we get to that, it is helpful to explore what we mean when we talk about the emotion of fear, because one of the more misunderstood relationships between emotional states is the one between fear and anxiety.

To understand fear we need to define it over and above other emotions we might experience. In a 2012 *New York Times* editorial, Joseph LeDoux admitted that "the line between fear and anxiety can get pretty thin and fuzzy."[11] This fuzzy line is seen in the language we use to talk about fearful and anxious experiences, mixing the two emotions as if they were completely interchangeable. To be sure, there are differences between fear and anxiety that are worth exploring.

A lot of our confusion probably stems from our adoption of psychological language into the everyday ways we talk to one another. The truth is, even in therapeutic circles, it is more common to discuss anxiety than fear. We put these two together, and often find ourselves mentioning anxiety when we mean fear and vice versa. While I will endeavor to define fear as different from anxiety, later chapters will be devoted to really teasing out what it means to be afraid and how that impacts our lives.

Since the turn of the twentieth century, when psychology became part of the social structure of various cultures, we have been trying to define humanity through a better understanding of the human brain and mind. We created a whole mess of words and concepts like *repression* (the stuffing of emotions or other painful experiences out of our consciousness) and *suppression* (the blocking of unacceptable desires from our consciousness) to describe our behaviors related to our thinking and experiencing of the world. Sometimes when we are trying to define a concept it is helpful to build our understanding through previous concepts. The difference between anxiety and fear is no exception. While anxiety has been preferred in certain therapy circles, some people have tried to describe the difference between the two emotional states.

The first description I want to point to is one from Seward Hiltner, a pastoral theologian:

[A] truer statement of the distinction in human beings between fear and anxiety would be to call the first the alarm signal that is read accurately without perceptible pause between signal and interpretation, while the latter involves perceptible pause.[12]

The way I read it, a perceptible pause is something akin to a reflection rather than a reaction. Thus anxiety involves at least a modicum of reflection before a response occurs. On the other hand, the emotion of fear is more reactive to a threat. Hiltner also uses the term *alarm signal*, which is certainly appropriate to both fear and anxiety. This may be another place where the two emotions become confused. Both signal a sense of unease about an experience, object, or relationship; however, fear provides a more immediate response to that experience while anxiety tends to encompass a reflective response. This of course does only a little bit to clear up the differences between anxiety and fear. So let's dive a little deeper.

Let's try and grasp the difference between these two emotions from the perspective of what is thought to provide healing. According to psychoanalyst Isaac Ramzy, "The simplest and the most accurate way of defining anxiety, however, is perhaps to contrast it with its opposite, which is peace—peace of the mind."[13] Therapists and other meditative specialists have often used a variety of peace-inducing techniques to help people cope with their anxieties. Peace, or engaging in peace-inducing activities, requires reflection; it requires training and practice and patience as we develop the skills to handle the anxieties that intrude on our lives. These are helpful skills to have when our lives are not directly threatened but instead overwhelmed by a general sense of unease. They are less helpful when we encounter a bear while walking through the woods.

I think a better antidote for fear is hope. Both fear and hope emotions have future-oriented components, and they are derived from connections to our memories, beliefs, and imaginations. To be hopeful in the face of an immediate threat is to give a sense of urgency to actions. Human beings have great survival instincts, but our emotional lives also give us the passion to know why living is important. Hope provides a more meaningful antidote to fear, as it directs us with the passion to thrive, giving us the reason to act upon the body's manifestation of fear.

Hiltner and Ramzy point us in two helpful directions concerning the emotion of fear. Their words about a perceptible pause and the role of peace help begin the process of separating fear and anxiety. Through them we begin to understand that anxiety most likely involves a reflective component that distinguishes it from fear. However, I think there is a more compelling argument to be made that can help us decide which emotion we are experiencing at different points in our lives. For that, I turn to psychologist Sonia Bishop, who defines the two terms this way:

> Fear is . . . a biologically adaptive physiological and behavioral response to the actual or anticipated occurrence of an explicit threatening stimulus. *Anxiety crucially involves uncertainty as to the expectancy of a threat, is triggered by less explicit or more generalized cues, and is characterized by a more diffuse state of distress, with symptoms of hyperarousal and worry.*[14]

The emotion of fear is generated by specific things. We fear something, someone, some imagined object. To be afraid means attaching an object to the emotion. I am afraid of spiders; I am anxious about watching my daughters grow up, date, and navigate the world. I hope you can see the difference here. Spiders are a definite object; they hold a place in my memory that signals danger whenever I see one. My anxiety about my daughters and their growth and development is a bit more mysterious and open-ended. Will they meet someone nice who treats them well? Will they be safe and secure? Will I be a good father? These kinds of questions lead to more generalized ruminations about possibilities of threatening experiences occurring in their lives.

As we can see, there are some differences that point to the uniqueness of each emotion. The place where this fuzzy line gets drawn is often with the personal experiences of each emotion. There is some crossover in the symptoms we experience in both emotions, such as hyperarousal or hypervigilance. However, when we think of anxiety and fear, we can also begin to talk about the intensity of experience. I surmise that things such as panic attacks often occur when we enter a generalized anxiety state and then become fixated on a particular object or thought that arouses the fear centers of our brains. This causes us to physically react in ways more akin to a fear response than an anxiety response. Generally speaking, the emotion of fear gives rise to specific behavioral responses such as fight, flight, freeze, and appease, whereas our anxieties most often produce a less-severe reaction to the generalized cues that make us worry.

One theory I have about this is that many of our anxieties stem from experiences of fear, held in our memories, which bleed out and get associated with new cues in our environments. This moves us to think about how the brain works. While the primary discussion on fear and the brain occurs in a later chapter, as I discuss the differences between fear and anxiety it is hard to do so without peering inside our skulls. Basically, I think of much of our anxiety as being generated by echoes of fear-associated memories, which in turn create an anticipation of possible dire consequences. In essence, fear-coded memories bleed out in a way that formerly specific threats are now associated with new and often undefined cues in the world. Some interesting research discusses the relationship between the amygdala and anxiety and fear.

The amygdalae are small almond-shaped clusters of neurons located in both "sides" of the brain just behind our eyes. Most neurological research points to these bundles of neurons as bearing responsibility for the emotion of fear. Additionally, some research shows that interaction between the amygdala and prefrontal circuits of the brain play a large role in anxiety production.[15] What this means is that the structure of the brain plays a big role in the production of fear and anxiety. Moreover, there are different sets of connections that are thought to produce each emotion. The amygdalae have some far-reaching connections with other parts of the brain, including those that store and produce memories. Part of the distinction between these two emotional states is how a stimulus is interpreted and the neural pathways that are engaged as a response.

Examining fear and anxiety, we can see that there is ample reason to think about them as distinct emotional states. They share some similarities, but ultimately are different emotions. Not including the different pathways engaged in the brain, four particular ideas help us understand this difference. Anxiety requires reflection; fear is more responsive. Peace is described as the antidote to anxiety; I believe the emotion of fear requires us to access a more hopeful imagination. The source of anxiety is often mysterious and open-ended; whereas with fear there is a specific object (real or imagined) attached to it. Finally, the resulting behaviors of each emotion differ, although there is some overlap here that often causes confusion.

Let's think back to Sandra's situation. She was mugged, and every ounce of her being felt the panic that comes from a surge of fear. In that moment she reacted to protect herself from the threat and to cope with what was happening to her. As she began to construct a future out of this experience, that fear-filled moment began to show up in a variety of settings. She interpreted sudden interruptions at her office as threats, staying hypervigilant in what had always been a safe place previously. She fled from situations that might cause her to react with fear. The difference between her reaction and one of pure anxiety was the hostile ways she began to interpret the world around her. A person only experiencing anxiety might be more cognizant of their surroundings; they might carry a whistle or pepper spray, but they still go out. A person experiencing a recurring sense of fear locks themselves away at night, or refuses to go out with friends; they may take the need to feel safe to an extreme rather than risk being hurt again.

We can see some of this in Jim's reaction to his fear as well. He took on the role of a protective aggressor. Even though his chances of being caught up in a terrorist plot were slim to none, he maintained the need to protect himself. This new worldview carried his actions to an extreme far beyond what might be considered a normal reaction to tragic events. Jim's choice was to fight in face of the things he feels threaten him. For someone who is afraid, this kind of behavior is not uncommon. The trouble for individuals and communities comes when it shapes the way we see the world; when we look into the future and threats dominate the landscape.

I think Jim and Sandra typify why theologians have been so afraid of the emotion of fear. It can wreak havoc on our lives and relationships. At the same time, the emotion of fear is incredibly adaptive. Fear is the emotional tool we use to survive, cope, and thrive in a sometimes hostile and unpredictable world. It is meant to be the trigger for a quick response to a threat, helping us act in particular ways when we face danger. Without fear, there is no humanity; there is no recognition of the will to live. Without fear, we walk up and pet lions and tigers and bears; without fear, we tiptoe to the edge of cliffs without a care about falling off; without fear, we miss the chance to reflect upon the possibilities to come, and we miss the opportunity to experience the things we hope for in life.

When the emotion of fear is utilized properly, it arises quickly as a reaction to a threat, and when that threat has abated it recedes into the background. In this way, the emotion of fear is one of the greatest gifts we have from God. It is the emotion that keeps us living; it is the state of being that helps us survive and cope in this world. We can make all of the theological arguments we want about God, embodiment, and the importance of emotions. However, the simple fact of the matter is that the emotion of fear has been conserved throughout our history to help us know when we need to protect our lives against the things that threaten us. For this gift, we should be grateful to God. Furthermore, trying to rid ourselves or suppress the emotion of fear seems counterproductive.

In Sandra's and Jim's cases, the emotion of fear shaped their world in drastic ways, which created hostility and isolation. This is why we need a better understanding of the emotion of fear from a theological point of view. How do you talk to Jim about the extreme measures he is taking? How do you help Sandra reclaim the goodness of life? The more we understand the emotion of fear and its complexities, the better we are able to see the concurrent stream of hope that flows with it. However, in this postmodern world, it is becoming increasingly hard to let our fears subside. As you will see in the next chapter, the threats we experience have been multiplying at an alarming rate, creating a Culture of Fear.

QUESTIONS FOR REFLECTION

1. How do you understand God? Does it help you to be able to think about God as a fellow sufferer who cares, or does this stretch your imagination too far?

2. What are the objects or specific things you fear? How do these things or experiences shape your behavior and relationships?

3. What do you imagine the connection between fear and hope to be as we think about faith and God?

Notes

1. Joseph E. LeDoux, *The Emotional Brain: The Mysterious Underpinnings of Emotional Life* (New York: Simon & Schuster Paperbacks, 1996), 16.

2. Ibid., 36.

3. I understand this term loosely as it relates to evolution and process theology, but can also respect its value in a variety of theological circles. However we might choose to interpret this phrase, to think of the *Imago Dei* as solely corporeal does it little justice. Moreover, thinking of it as a purely rational image may go too far as well. To truly understand the *Imago Dei*, we must look beyond human constructions and capabilities—our physical attributes, mental capacities, and even emotional abilities—and peer into the mystery of love, grace, justice, and hope. These thematic images form a more consistent understanding of God that reveals an active relational power and presence to the world. Thus to be in the image of God is to act, feel, and think in ways that embody the attributes we ascribe to the Holy Other. In this way, emotions become central to the *Imago Dei* rather than an afterthought.

4. Robert Thompson, "Process Theology and Emotion: An Introductory Exploration," *Journal of Pastoral Theology* 15, no. 1 (2005): 19.

5. Ibid., 28.

6. You can look to the second chapter in Exodus to see this kind of empathic response play out; additionally, the Psalms (such as Psalm 40) and prophets (such as Isaiah 58) are sources where you see reference to God's hearing and responding to the cries of oppressed, lonely, and lost people. To be fair, there are also passages that allude to God's hiddenness. Yet, even these passages have hints of anger or other emotions that drive the passion of God elsewhere.

7. Carrie Doehring, *The Practice of Pastoral Care: A Postmodern Approach* (Louisville: Westminster John Knox, 2006), 18.

8. Ibid., 25.

9. This includes thinking about what we would consider to be the core emotions conserved in the structures of the brain. Jaak Panksepp, a psychologist and neuroscientist, says that "[p]rimary emotional systems, as far as we know, are intrinsic within brain tools for allowing animals to generate complex, dynamically flexible instinctual action patterns to cope with specific environmental enticements and threats" (2007, p. 1821). Early lists of primary emotions generally posited four: mad, sad, glad, and afraid. As modern neuroscience helps us better understand the capacities of the brain, ideas about the shape of our emotions have changed. Categories like

primary, secondary, universal, etc. have been proposed with some fanfare, but often without the kind of support needed to establish a true taxonomy of emotions. That said, neuropsychologists today often describe seven arguable, but identifiable, emotional states: care, play, panic, rage, seeking, fear, lust (Panksepp, 2007, p. 1825). Jaak Panksepp, "Criteria for Basic Emotions: Is DISGUST a Primary 'Emotion'?," *Cognition & Emotion* 21, no. 8 (2007): 1819–28.

10. Here, I am reminded of my first class in my doctoral program. We were discussing what we can and cannot claim about God. One student's position was that we cannot have any ultimate claims about the true nature of God. This is true to a certain extent. The understanding that I came to, after conversation with Larry Kent Graham, was that God gave us brains that reason, experience, emote, and imagine. If we do not use these capabilities to their fullest, we don't do God any favors. Therefore, we should question and assert in conversation and collaboration to develop ideas about God that stretch our understanding and challenge any stagnant beliefs. Once this has been done, we can leave the rest to mystery.

11. Joseph E. LeDoux, "Searching the Brain for the Roots of Fear," *New York Times*, January 22, 2012, http://opinionator.blogs.nytimes.com/2012/01/22/anatomy-of-fear/?hp.

12. Seward Hiltner, "Some Theories of Anxiety: Psychiatric," in *Constructive Aspects of Anxiety*, ed. Seward Hiltner and Karl Menninger (New York: Abingdon, 1960), 47.

13. Isaac Ramzy, "Freud's Understanding of Anxiety," in *Constructive Aspects of Anxiety*, ed. Seward Hiltner and Karl Menninger (New York: Abingdon, 1960), 18.

14. Sonia J. Bishop, "Neurocognitive Mechanisms of Anxiety: An Integrative Account," *Trends in Cognitive Sciences* 11, no. 7 (2007): 307.

15. See Bishop, "Neurocognitive Mechanisms of Anxiety: An Integrative Account," 307–16, and R. J. Davidson, "Anxiety and Affective Style: Role of Prefrontal Cortex and Amygdala," *Biological Psychiatry* 51, no. 1 (2002): 68–80, for a broader understanding of the interaction between the amygdala and the rest of the brain in the production of anxiety and fear.

2

A Culture of Fear

*We would like to remind you that the
current terror alert level is orange . . .
Tonight, on the news, a group of teenagers
was caught on camera beating a man
downtown . . .
If you vote for this president, then the
terrorists win . . .
If we continue to consume our energy
resources at this pace, we will decimate
the earth . . .*

Fear permeates the fabric of our lives. Walking through the airport we hear a familiar and a soothing voice come over the loudspeaker claiming, "The terror alert level has been raised to orange." We surf the Internet, and casually catch headlines that declare economic breakdowns, bombings in various countries, or the latest natural disaster. We flip through the television channels and catch a teaser for the evening news declaring a murder, rape, or burglary in a neighborhood close to us. We look out the window and see a strange man walk by our house; so we grab the phone and check the door to make sure it is locked. Passive and active acceptance of the importance of terror, crime, and strangers lend credence to the establishment of a culture of fear in the United States.

When we are fed a steady diet of threats, it often feels like there is little recourse other than to live in fear of the world around us. Now that we have a sense of the difference between fear and anxiety, it is important to understand why this difference matters. In our current culture, I believe we find ourselves experiencing pervasive amounts of fear and anxiety. These possibilities invade our lives through the airwaves, the Internet, and our interactions with others.

Remember, the emotion of fear needs a specific object, whether real or imagined. To be afraid is to be afraid of something. We can fear spiders or snakes, terrorists or tornados, crime or almost any manner of object that has been tagged in our memories as worthy of fearing. Think about your context for a moment, the places you live, the people you know, the news you hear or read, and your reactions to them all. As you take in the world and understand the difference between fear and anxiety, can you begin to see how they impact our lives?

The poet W. H. Auden, in *The Age of Anxiety*, described the world as a constantly changing landscape where technology and industrialization wreak havoc on our sense of meaning. Psychologists and sociologists often describe us as living under successive ages of anxiety. One Slovenian philosopher remarked that "[w]hen we talk about the new age of anxiety we should not forget that in the last century it was always the case that after some major social crisis there came the age of anxiety."[1] However, even as she begins talking about these new ages of anxiety, she notes the difference in the most recent social crises. She believes that fear is being peddled in the marketplace. She points to the September 11th attacks and notes that "[a]fter September 11 the American government has been keeping the fear of possible new attacks alive by continuously reminding the public of the unpredictable danger that can come from hidden terrorists."[2] Even as I write these words eleven years later, I am reminded of a recent trip through the airport. Wandering to my flight, the background noise was punctuated by announcements of those color-coded threat levels. In all of my years flying since that fateful day in 2001, I don't think that I have ever experienced a threat level below orange in an airport. Of course the orange threat level is one color away from red, and the message of an impending terrorist attack. What I conclude is that I am supposed to be afraid when I fly, that when I wander through an airport I am to engage in the kind of hypervigilance that fear engenders.

We are given threat levels in the interest of public safety. However, their effect is to create a sense of hyperarousal about our surroundings, to remind us of the imminence of possible threats. As we walk into an airport we are simply told to be afraid, that danger lurks with every stranger or backpack or person who looks different than ourselves. This is what begins to separate a mere age of anxiety from a culture of fear. We are fed a steady diet of tangible threats with which to imagine our demise. Specific objects are held in our collective memory and our response together becomes one of fear rather than anxiety.

While it is not easy to dismiss the ages of anxiety that persist, anxiety is not a rich enough word to describe the collective emotions we experience and act upon today. As you read this chapter, think about the implicit messages about threats that you hear on a daily basis. What kind of outlook does this create for you? How do you react to the threats peddled in the common space of our life together? We are going to explore the meaning of the phrase *culture of fear*, its roots and causes, and what it means to our communities and relationships with one another. As we do so, how do you understand yourself as complicit in or resistant to these forces in your life?

A Culture of Fear

Cultures are often defined by a persistent set of rules and behaviors that set them apart from other groups. Culture also becomes defined and described by our relationships with particular people, objects, or experiences. Institutions have cultures; societies have cultures; families have cultures, as do businesses, churches, nations, and so forth. Thus when we think of something like a culture of fear, there has to be some kind of broad pattern or acceptance of this emotional state as it orients our actions and reactions. *Culture of fear* describes an underlying pattern of behavior related to the emotion of fear that is seen in how we interact and interrelate with the world around us.[3]

Looking at the context of the United States in particular, we seem to have stepped beyond merely being anxious about an uncertain future. A constant stream of threats rises and falls throughout the days of our lives. We are told what is happening in the world, and many of us draw in these experiences and events, and breathe out fear and worry. Speaking about the culture in the United States, theologian Kirk Bingaman describes it this way:

> Fear mongers, in droves, heighten our levels of anxiety by offering us a pessimistic view of the future. Unless we do what they tell us and return to a set of values or a system of belief or meaning largely derived from the past, the future, so they say, does not look very promising.[4]

Looking at his words, we see the interaction between fear and anxiety rise again. Bingaman is essentially making the argument for a new age of anxiety, one that is punctuated by persistent fears. I am taking things a step further, seeking to open our eyes to the culture of fear created by our extensive exposure to threats. For me, the rise of imagined and experienced threats generates the emotion of fear to such a level that it affects our cultural and relational structure.

Fear is an adaptive emotion, one that is protective and life-saving in most instances. However, we have probably all experienced how our emotions can be manipulated. We have watched movies that make us cry with joy or sadness, or heard stories that made us seethe with anger. The manipulation of our emotions and ability to connect with experiences has long been a tool of movies and television. People who study social phenomena believe that the emotion of fear is one of the primary emotions manipulated by people in power, or those who want it. For example:

> Creating and sustaining this fear serves some of the most powerful interests in American society. The media are interested in cultivating fear because it sells more ads and publications. The more afraid people are, the more information they crave. Politicians are interested in cultivating fear because it provides fertile ground to offer solutions. The more afraid people are, the more they crave solutions to the problem. . . . Commercial interests also benefit as people seek goods and services to make them safer. Finally, various governmental institutions benefit as they receive more funding to take care of the problem.[5]

Think about this for a moment: there are powerful interests in the world that require us to be afraid. Therefore, they carefully craft a message that will raise our awareness about a threat they create. Knowing that the emotion of fear is a potent emotion that can direct our actions, they utilize this to make us buy in to an argument, or just buy something in particular. While anxiety creates unease about the future, fear sells the knowledge of specific threats, and it sells solutions to alleviate our discomfort in being afraid. We use the emotion of fear to sell survival gear; we use it to sell suspicion of our neighbors; we use it to convert and save souls; we use it to create positive and negative ideas about different cultures and nations.

The emotion of fear is a powerful motivator; it drives us to act. Most often, fear is adaptive, helping us creatively engage an experience and develop results for our continued safety and life. Fear is meant to arise and abate. However, the current cultural milieu creates, if we let it, a fear that seeps into the fabric of our lives, creating background noise that orients us to the world in ways that disrupt relationships and flavor our interpretations of events around us.

Selling Fear

There are myriad ways that the emotion of fear is sold on the open market. Three strike me as important examples. Terrorism has become a hallmark of the selling of fear in the United States. Since the September 11th attacks[6] we have been fed a steady stream of terrorist talk. Locally, our news programs, online media, and stories often revolve around the prevalence of crime in the areas we live. Finally, there is an overarching sense of stranger danger that permeates the relationships we have and/or attempt to form. Taken together, these three examples develop a picture concerning what it means to live in a culture of fear.

Terrorism—the very moniker is meant to invoke the experience of fear. It has the power to halt air travel; the power to make countries spend themselves into bankruptcy; the power to keep us at home and keep us suspicious of our neighbors and others who might seem different. Terrorism, and safety from it, is what we appeal to when we need to usurp the rights of individuals or incarcerate people indefinitely. Since 2001, terrorism is a communal term that has personal meaning meant to call forth the memories of the events of 9/11, and it is used in overt and covert ways to define how we are supposed to act and react to the world around us.

The overt methods of speaking about terrorism are easy to spot, though their impact may be more subtle. The constant news about plots that are hatched and/or foiled keeps the prospect of a threat on our minds. Political parties invoke terrorist events before they announce policies that curtail civil liberties or restrict movement. With a desire for greater safety, we applaud these ideas as patriotic and smart, hoping to catch "bad" guys, and overlooking the innocent people who get caught up or profiled by these new restrictions.

Think a bit about the years following the September 11th attacks. Consider, for example, what psychologists Konty, Duell, and Joireman say about the era:

> A daily diet of color-coded warnings and announcements that this or that building is under threat. . . . Politicians engaged the "politics of fear" (Altheide, 2004) to push through emergency legislation giving control agents more authority to investigate and prevent further attacks and giving the executive branch the authority to use the military as it sees fit. Commercial interests rushed to market products to keep the public safe. Products not previously in demand—gas masks and sealable rooms to guard against biological or chemical weapons, parachutes and inflatable slides to escape from high rises under attack, giant bomb-detecting machines for airports and important buildings—now found a hungry market. New governmental institutions were formed and given tremendous power and oversight. New federal workers in the airports require

babies and old ladies to present their shoes for inspection while stray bags are destroyed with explosives.[7]

Most of these new policies and institutions now work in the background of our lives. We wander through airports noting, but not necessarily noticing, the impact of a calm terror-warning level announcement. We tacitly accept new levels of invasive monitoring in our lives in the interest of public safety and good. Paralyzed by the possibility of terror, we grumble, but in the end nod our heads in acceptance of political rhetoric that labels and demonizes groups of people for the sins of a few. On a national scale, there is a constant message that we are to remain vigilant, and the best way to do that is ensure that we experience a pervasive low level of fear such that we are always ready to jump at the slight possibility of danger. I think that if we were to begin to examine the headlines and the messages they convey, we would begin to see how the emotion of fear is being manipulated to keep us from engaging in the world in hopeful and meaningful ways.

Terrorism is but one term used to keep us on our fearful best. When you add in constant reporting of global catastrophes—of hurricanes, floods, tornadoes, and tsunamis—we have a growing awareness that our world is hostile and unpredictable. These events are at our fingertips as reporters are sent into the eyes of the storms in order to bring back images that haunt our lives. We have instant access to terrifying events, as they occur, that create a picture of an unsafe and dangerous world. These events create a semi-permanent state of unrest related to the emotion of fear. They form a curtain of background noise and engender a state of fear that makes us more prone to specific behavioral responses that are predictable and easy to manipulate at times.

While terrorism and global disasters provide a global backdrop to influence our emotional interactions with the world, crime provides us with another source of fear that is more local and possibly more sinister. Think for a moment about your evening news or the RSS feed that pushes the top stories on the Internet to your desktop. What information is being pushed into your lives about the world, your local area, and even your hometown? If you still watch the evening news, what are the headlined stories that attempt to grab your attention? Usually the top story relates to a crime (real threat) or conspiracy (imagined threat). These teasers about the threats in our midst give us pause as we go about our days. We wonder if a stranger in our midst is going to hurt us. We tell ourselves that he looks like the mug shot on television or the front page, and that we best be wary. We create connections between people's outward appearance and preformed ideas about their actions. Crime, and the associations our imaginations make regarding it, impacts our ability to be relational people in this world.

Konty, Duell, and Joireman state that "[f]ear is a relational product"; therefore, "when a social relation is structured such that one entity has the power to dictate the outcome of a second party, the second party will experience fear."[8] These same authors, looking at a variety of studies on crime, find that the more you know about crime, the more likely you are to fear it. They describe three attitudes that result from increased knowledge of crime.

First, knowledge of crime leads us to distrust our neighbors. Think about where you live. How many people around you do you know? According to these authors,

> [p]eople who fear crime are less likely to venture beyond their front doors thus constraining their interactions with others. Research in fact demonstrates a clear inverse relationship between community integration and the fear of crime. Where community integration is high, the fear of crime is low.[9]

Now, certainly there are some neighbors we are better off not knowing. For the most part though, we tend to feel safer, as though our house is a home, when we know the people around us. Life becomes a little more predictable and we can feel a little safer knowing that we are known. The more we know about and fear crime, the less likely we are to approach our neighbors and get to know them. Unknown people become "others" rather than persons, and we assume that something about them is not worth trusting.

Next, the more we know about crime, the more likely we are to want harsh punishments related to it. As we hear about crimes in our areas, we believe that we will feel safer when people are put away. We prefer simple solutions rather than thinking about the complex situations through which some crimes arises. This is a function of feeling afraid. When we are afraid, we tend to focus on the simple solutions that are needed to remedy the emotions we are feeling. Instead of thinking about the oppression that some feel in our society, or the ways that politicians, pundits, and news sources simplify cases, we tend toward simple right or wrong solutions that may or may not work in all cases.

The final attitude that is borne out of a knowledge of crime is one that I want to explore a little more. Namely, that crime restricts social behavior. To fear crime is to isolate oneself from the greater community, believing and acting in a manner that sees the possible criminal in every person just waiting to get out. It is not to anticipate apprehensively that one might become a victim of crime, but to act in manner where we believe that our victimization is inevitable. Anxiety turns on the outside lights and locks the doors; fear bolts bars to windows and buys a handgun to place under the pillow. This attitude comes from our imagination. The more we hear about crime, the more we imagine it is going to happen to us. Sociologist Zygmunt Bauman explored the intersection of the emotion of fear and our imaginations. Using the trial of Adolf Eichmann, who was tried and convicted as a Nazi war criminal, he examined how fear can weave its way into our relationships, or potential relationships with others.

Psychiatrists who interviewed Eichmann described him as normal, as someone who even displayed many desirable qualities as a family man. They talked about him as

> an unexceptional, dull, boringly "ordinary" creature: someone you pass on a street without noticing. As a husband, father or neighbour he would hardly stand out from the crowd. . . . He just, as we all do, preferred his own comfort to that of others. It is that common, *ordinary* malfeasance or lapse that at an *extra*ordinary time leads to *extra*ordinary results.[10]

At the end of the day, Eichmann's psychological makeup was not much different than our own. According to Bauman, Eichmann was not so much evil incarnate as a product of his context and his desire for self-preservation, which suggests that all of us are capable of evil acts when our desire for self-preservation is manipulated under the right circumstances. This is probably the greatest threat we face in terms of social behavior. If seemingly normal people like ourselves can do evil things, then how much more evil can be perpetrated by a stranger who seems to be normal as well? As Bauman says, "Trust is in trouble the moment we know that evil may hide *anywhere*; that it does not stand out from the crowd, does not bear distinctive marks and carries no identity card."[11]

Now it is vital to realize that not everyone commits such atrocities, even under extreme circumstances like those of Nazi Germany. A great many people resisted the impulse to commit heinous acts against their fellow human beings, and not every German became Adolf Eichmann when presented with the opportunity. However, what this teaches us about humanity—and this is amplified in the media—is that ordinary people do extraordinarily bad things sometimes. We constantly hear stories of people's lives where the tagline is that they always seemed so normal. Even our churches with their focus on sin at times point to our worst fears—namely, that within each of us is the ability to produce great evil.

The seemingly natural result is to live carefully, trusting few and fearing most. We end up listening to the nightly news, the Internet, or even the sirens of passing police cars, only to confirm our suspicions about our fears and the unpredictable world full of people out there. Actually, it becomes predictable in the sense that we develop values around the idea that everyone else poses a tangible threat, and that we must do what we can to prevent our fears from becoming real.

Bauman calls this "derivative fear,"

> the sentiment of being *susceptible* to danger; a feeling of insecurity (the world is full of dangers that may strike at any time with little or no warning) and vulnerability (in the event of danger striking, there will be little if any chance of escape or successful defence; the assumption of vulnerability to dangers depends more on a lack of trust in the defences available than on the volume or nature of actual threats.[12]

Basically, this is the idea that we soak up the threats from our surroundings—the media, the experiences, the values—and develop a preemptive sense of fear. It is not the anticipation that something unknown will happen to us. It is the anticipation of a particular threat—crime, terrorism, a natural disaster, or an individual harming us. Thus we become preoccupied with safety and security and orient our lives and values to the alleviation of these feelings of discord in our lives.

Insecurity and vulnerability become synonyms for helplessness and powerless. The susceptibility to danger Bauman describes feeds a culture of fear, and makes it all but certain that our ages of anxiety will persist indefinitely. Thus when we dare walk into the dangerous world, we do so in fear. At a basic level, we operate under the notion that threats are probable at worst and possible at best. As Bauman points out, "occasions to be afraid are one of the few things of which our times, badly missing certainty, security and safety, are not short. Fears are many and varied."[13] Furthermore, our fears feed a sense of impotence, which Bauman calls "that most frightening impact of fear."[14] Thus we not only live among all these threats; the constant reminder of them has the possibility of rendering us powerless to stop a threat should it arise. As we are increasingly subjected to global tragedy, global warming, global pandemics, and other global threats, there is a "tendency to perceive human activity through a narrative that emphasizes its selfish, destructive and toxic behavior [which] underpins our culture of fear."[15]

More than just the powerless feelings we sometimes experience in the face of a threat, the constant reminders create a worldview that, over time, becomes fear-based. The constant awareness of threats feeds our imaginations and forces us into particular perspectives about the world and its inhabitants. Sociologist Frank Furedi remarks that our current cultural milieu encourages "an expansive alarmist imagination through providing the public with a steady diet of fearful programmes about impending calamities—man-made and natural."[16] As we hear about pandemic flus, tsunamis, crime, and the normalcy of people who commit heinous crimes, our imaginations begin to kick in to overdrive. Our attention is aroused and we create ideas, which become certainties in our minds, about the calamities that will definitely impact us. It's not that every stranger on the street might do something to harm us, but in our minds we are convinced that strangers are threats to us, until proven otherwise.

Individual interpretations of media and relationships are a big part of how we come to understand the world. Think about the world and the people you know. How do they/you filter the information presented? How do you parse what is a meaningful threat versus what can be ignored? Moreover, how does your interaction with these threats impact your relationships with others? Living and interacting through a fear-based worldview is exhausting. Even just reading this, I imagine that you might be throwing your hands in the air, either in frustration, anger, or exasperation. My guess is that you have furiously scribbled in the margins points of agreement or disagreement.

The bleak assessment of the current cultural milieu by sociologists and psychologists points to the reality of fear as a worldview creator. It is enough to make us long for simpler days, enough to make us want to disconnect from the world and live in isolation from the threats it presents. While we can certainly escape the presentation of threats, we cannot escape the embodied emotion of fear. This is why it is more helpful to understand how fear impacts our lives in complex ways. Rather than sweep it under the rug with platitudes and simplicity, we are required to think differently about the embodiment of fear and its social prevalence, and to respond accordingly.

My sense is that much of Christian theology is predicated on the possibility of hope. What I propose here seems to negate or diminish the possibility of hope in our lives. As a pastoral theologian, I consider much of my work to be concerned with the restoration of hope in an unpredictable and sometimes hostile world. I see hope as a fundamental orientating paradigm to life-giving theologies. Too often, our theologies hinge on the ability to coerce people into believing particular ideas through fear; we forget the role of hope, grace, and love. Without hope, the possibilities of love and grace as practical acts of faith lose their flavor and meaning. Hope reveals our sense that the world can be a better place, that people can relate more meaningfully, and that God is present, active, and caring. My promise to you is that over the course of this book we will get there. Not by ignoring the reality of fear, or going back to simple "do not fear" statements. Instead we will get there by leaning in to what the emotion of fear can teach us about life. We will get there by seeing fear as complex, as something that is conserved throughout our evolving history, as something indicating a great human will to survive, cope, and thrive in a world of possible threats.

LOOKING BACK AT JIM

Think back to Jim's reaction to the world around him, his concern with safety and security and his alienation from people in the community. His actions and thoughts reveal someone who seems afraid. He is guarded; his behavior, though perfectly rational to him, seems out of kilter with those around him. Jim is not just anxious about an uncertain future, he is afraid of the threats he believes surround him at every turn. This is the kind of behavior that a culture of fear inculcates.

We all know people like Jim; they may have slightly different foci or display varying degrees of fear. They might be wary of others, or constantly vigilant; some may even buy in to the need to purchase devices meant to ensure their safety and security, or they seem to push people away or separate themselves from others. As much as we can point to the "Jims" in our lives, at times we may even act in the same way. We hear the language used to describe strangers; we become self-preserving, sometimes at the expense of others. It is easy to absorb the threats presented by the world and react with separation and suspicion. People living in fear sit in the pews of churches; they run sessions and boards; they are our elders and deacons, our ushers and volunteers. As you read this, think about your own context for a moment. Have you noticed a change in behavior in the folks you minister to? How would you describe it?

If we truly look, I think what we will see is behavior that steps beyond mere worry. We might see people using language that separates and divides; they might talk about mundane things in suspicious ways. Purveyors of fear feed upon our imaginations by sensationalizing events and presenting opinion as fact. They transform a sometimes hostile world into a place of definite danger; they turn unpredictability into catastrophe and life into a minefield. Rather than awakening each morning to the possibility of creativity and novelty, we are introduced to a battlefield we have little hope of navigating without their particular solution.

In fact, after reading this you may feel a little wary yourself. Even just calling attention to the emotion of fear can make us aware of its presence, or remind us of threats we face or have faced. Actually, this is good. It is good to face down the things that scare the wits out of us. It is good to know and name those objects in our lives. Without naming and claiming certain things, we give our imaginations free rein to embellish their impact on our lives. If we admonish ourselves not to fear in the face of danger or threats, we lose a vital way of interacting with the world. In this climate of fear, the arousal of this powerful emotion is taken too far. Part of calling attention to a culture of fear is seeing it as an opportunity to evaluate the veracity of imagined threats. Another part is to develop a complex sense of the meaning of fear so that we can experience it as a gift and understand its value and relationship to hope.

There are places in this world that experience real threats on a constant basis. Truth be told, the United States is not often one of those places. However, we often react to what we see, hear, and read as though the world is dangerous to our health. Suddenly, the young mother in our community refuses to have her child immunized because of a pumped-up story in the news (despite much evidence to corroborate the safety of immunizations). The grandmother in your congregation starts sending inflammatory emails to the staff, filled with half-truths about specific populations of people. Normally thoughtful people react angrily to a sermon that seems to take a political position contrary to their own. The leadership in your community of faith reacts with extreme prejudice when one of the youth announces that he or she is gay. All of these things can be reactions based on fear. When something threatens us, we often attempt to preserve our self and sense of life.

All of this may have you saying, "The scripture was right, do not fear is the way to go." Unfortunately, this is impossible. We are built, by God, to experience the emotion of fear. At the same time, we were built for love, hope, sadness, peace, anger, and joy. In a world where the dissemination of threats is the status quo, we need a constructive and complex view of fear so that we can wholly faithful to our embodied, spiritual, psychological selves.

As you continue to read, become aware of the people around you and the language they use to describe the world.

QUESTIONS FOR REFLECTION

1. How do the people around you interact with strangers?

2. What is your/their reaction to natural disasters or other intrusive surprising events?
3. Think about the communities of faith you attend and work for. What is their reaction to the changing environment? How do you/they react to events that challenge their theology or worldview?
4. As they/you interact with the world, what habits are you developing that are meant to preserve a personal sense of safety and security? How do these habits impact the whole community of faith?

Notes

1. Renata Salecl, *On Anxiety* (London: Routledge, 2004), 1.
2. Ibid., 7.
3. I speak from the context of a United States citizen, and I imagine this context as more relevant to others who would describe themselves similarly. It's not that this work has no merit in other parts of the world; it is more a recognition that I see this culture operating in this specific context. For you, and the places you live and move and become, a culture of fear may be present and manifest in different ways.
4. Kirk A. Bingaman, *Treating the New Anxiety: A Cognitive-Theological Approach* (Lanham, MD: Jason Aronson, 2007), 57.
5. Mark Konty, Blythe Duell, and Jeff Joireman, "Scared Selfish: A Culture of Fear's Values in the Age of Terrorism," *The American Sociologist* 35, no. 2 (Summer 2004): 94.
6. I think it is important to recognize that there is a moderately credible threat here. However, most people in this country are not in a place where they could be directly impacted by a terrorist threat. Most people in the United States live in relative safety and comfort compared to countries where this type of threat is a real and sometimes daily occurrence. I think of the September 11th attacks as an event that marked a turning point in the United States toward a more overt culture of fear. Terrorism is a disgusting form of social action, often with the intent of harming people to make a political point. At the same time, our reaction of anger and hostility may do more harm than good. While I am not necessarily advocating a pacifist position, I do think that we could reflect more on the politics of the world and respond in faithful ways that demand accountability and justice when such atrocities are committed.
7. Ibid., 95.
8. Ibid., 96.
9. Ibid., 95–96.
10. Zygmunt Bauman, *Liquid Fear* (Cambridge: Polity Press, 2006), 67.
11. Ibid., 67.
12. Ibid., 3 (italics author's).
13. Ibid., 20.
14. Ibid.
15. Frank Furedi, *Culture of Fear Revisited: Risk-Taking and the Morality of Low Expectation*, 4th ed. (London: Continuum, 2006), xiv.
16. Ibid., viii.

PART 2

What Does It Mean to Be Afraid?

We all experience fear, and the current theological tools and interpretations do little justice to this adaptable emotion. In Part 1 we explored how we have divorced emotional experiences from our concepts of God and thus how it impacts our faith. In describing the difference between fear and anxiety, we began to make the conversation about our emotional lives a bit more complex. This led to a discussion about the current culture of fear that seems to pervade our lives through the media. These discussions help us describe why it is important to tackle the emotion of fear through a theological lens.

In part 2, we turn to exploring the "how." The next two chapters explore fear in both individual and communal contexts. Chapter 3 looks at the embodied and embedded aspects of fear. It explores how the brain generates fear, as well as how our memories encode certain experiences with the emotion of fear; this is the most technical chapter in this book. Any attempt to explain neuropsychological research using colloquial language is bound to leave things out or over simplify an argument. Where necessary I have commented further in the notes or offered resources to explore.

Chapter 4 revolves around a case study meant to help us understand how the stories we tell and share can create a fear-based communal narrative. This chapter begins by exploring the ways the emotion of fear can be transmitted through nonverbal cues. As you explore these chapters, continue to keep your own context in mind. Part of our exploration into the emotion of fear is understanding how it comes to be expressed personally and also in the communities where we dwell.

3

Our Frightened Brains

Simply put, I am afraid of spiders. I can remember countless experiences when I have been surprised by the appearance of spider and reacted in less-than-rational ways. While I wouldn't describe myself as phobic, I do observe myself as more vigilant than most others in spaces where spiders are known to dwell. Part of the joke in our house is that our marriage vows included the agreement that my spouse would deal with spiders; I would handle the other bugs in our home. While there are a number of ways to look at this fear (and most might involve a long course of therapy), there are two particular things we should note. The first is to explore what happens to the brain and body when a threat arises. The second is to examine how spiders become an object that I fear.

Neuropsychologists Johnson and LeDoux talk about fear using two lenses. They state that there are the "subjective states (the feeling of fear) and bodily responses (behavioral, autonomic, and endocrine changes) elicited by threatening stimuli."[1] In this chapter we will use the terms *embodied* and *embedded* to describe the different ways of comprehending the emotion of fear. Thus there is fear, and there are fears. The first, *fear*, describes the embodied, or physiological, component of being afraid. Much of this is governed by particular clusters of neurons in the brain that are interconnected to other systems in the body. The second, *fears*, describes the embedded component of being afraid—the unique things we are conditioned to fear. These objects are derived from our experiences, memories, beliefs, and the ways we imagine the world working.

Seeing fear this way reminds me of dual-inheritance evolutionary theory. Philosopher Stefan Linquist describes this model thusly:

> The key idea is that complex psychological traits are transmitted from parent to offspring via two parallel channels. The computational "hardware" required for social learning is transmitted

genetically and the psychological "software" that supports a given technology or skill is transmitted culturally.[2]

Much like embedded (subjective) and embodied (physiological), the hardware-software approach to evolution helps us understand the ubiquitous and unique ways emotions impact our lives. Thus emotions are embodied; they are part of our genetic code and physiological makeup, conserved in our evolutionary history.[3] This is what gives all of us the capacity to experience the emotion of fear (along with other emotions). On the other hand, emotions are embedded as well; their triggers are unique from person to person. Due to our experiences in this world—the places we live, the people we grow up living around, and our unique way of creatively interpreting the environment—we fear different things with differing levels of intensity.

Opening the evolutionary can of worms in this way allows us to see the emotion of fear as both efficient and flexible—efficient in the sense that fear and its accompanying behaviors have been honed and shaped through successive generations of life; flexible with the understanding that fear is shaped by culture and experience. I fear spiders while you might fear heights or snakes, terrorists, or crime, even small spaces or large crowds. Although the specific objects we fear are unique to us, the neurological and behavioral reactions share a good bit of similarity.

THE EMBODIED EMOTION OF FEAR

As we discussed earlier, many of our emotional states are embodied aspects of our brains. Try as we might, we cannot escape, rationalize, or completely extinguish the emotion of fear from our lives. Our embodied selves are vital to the ways we interact with the world around us. We are meaning-making creatures who experience the world corporeally. Think about that for a moment. We are people who interact with the world; we take in sensory data, process it, interpret it, and act upon the meanings and values we place upon these experiences. All of this happens in the context of our physical selves—brains, bodies, and minds included.

Talking about the brain, the initial locus for the rise of our emotions and thoughts has rarely been a high priority for theologians. We use our brains all the time (although that may be debatable to some) to interpret and create meaning from our experiences. We use our brains to create sermons, to drive our cars to work, to walk, to talk, to breathe, to see, and so on. However, a novel task for those of us who think faith is important may be to see the brain and brain research as primary components in a theological anthropology. Our humanity, arguably, depends upon our neurophysiology. The brain is the seat of interpretation, memory, imagination, emotions, and thoughts; and perhaps more importantly, it regulates our physical selves. Any time we begin to speculate about humanity, we should pay attention to what we are learning about the brain. At the same time, we should see this research tentatively, knowing that we are merely at the beginning stages of describing the wonders the brain contains. So, with the stage set, let's turn to looking at the embodiment of fear and how that plays out through particular physical reactions.

When I say that I am afraid of spiders, what does that mean? In terms of the brain, it means that when something resembling a spider peripherally enters my senses, a series of reactions occurs. My brain attempts to identify the object while simultaneously preparing my body to react as though it is a spider. As this fast path to fear engages, a slightly slower path (think milliseconds here) searches my memories for past experiences of similar objects. This type of reaction ensures that I am prepared if the object turns out to be a spider, or mitigates the fear response if it turns out to be a dust bunny rolling across the floor. As you can see, a number of interconnected parts of the brain engage when the possibility of a threat arises.

Taking a closer look at this process, the rise of fear most often begins with sensory data. This means that often it is something in the environment that triggers the emotion of fear. The tricky piece is that the object we experience may have nothing to do with the actual object we are afraid of. Think about hearing a car backfire, which might trigger a memory of a gunshot, and send us scrambling to the floor. It could be a vertigo-inducing picture that reminds us of a fear of heights, which in turn triggers a minor physical response. These embedded fears often have wide-ranging triggers that call forth the embodied emotion of fear. We are getting a little bit ahead of ourselves, but it is important to realize that it is our relationship to specific objects that most often triggers the emotion of fear. The good news is that while we experience a modicum of fear in those moments, it usually quickly dissipates as we come to recognize what is actually there.

As we experience a trigger for the emotion of fear, the brain begins to process the data it has received. The part of the brain that is most associated with the emotion of fear is the amygdala. Joseph LeDoux, a neuropsychologist who has spent much of his life studying fear, says that "[t]he key to the fear pathways in the brain is a small region called the amygdala."[4] The amygdala is a small bilateral (meaning it has two parts, one in each hemisphere of the brain) almond-shaped bundle of neurons. Put your fingers on your temple, and then imagine a spot directly behind your eyes intersecting where your fingers are pointing; that is the approximate location of the amygdala. The amygdala is a well-connected bundle of neurons. It is directly connected to the thalamus, which is the direct receptor of all that sensory data we experience. Furthermore, it is connected to our cortical structures, which is where a lot of our reasoning and memory functions lie.[5] These two different pathways connecting to the amygdala allow us to immediately prepare to act in the face of a threat, even while we are still assessing the extent of the threat itself.

The amygdala also connects to parts of the brain responsible for physical activity (the autonomic system). Thus when we experience what we think is a threat, several things occur. The first thing that happens is our attention is drawn to the object; we become hyper-focused on what we believe is a threat. In that moment of focusing, we briefly freeze as our blood flow increases, our heart pounds, and our body tenses. We become pale as a ghost in these moments as the blood drains from our faces and into our muscles, readying them for a defensive movement. We might feel our mouths turn dry as our digestive system shuts down to conserve energy. Furthermore, a rush of hormones enters our bloodstream, heightening our sensitivity to the world around us. All of this happens in milliseconds as the brain searches our memories in order to recognize the object or experience before us. If what we are experiencing is a threat, then the body goes into action, utilizing a prescribed set of possible defensive behaviors.

It is the defensive behaviors resulting from the emotion of fear that are probably most familiar to us. We can most likely name each one by heart: *flight, fight, freeze,* and *appease.* Each behavior is unique in that it arises in order to enable us to survive, cope, and thrive in this sometimes hostile world. I also think our general reaction to fear often stems from its integrated behaviors, which often feel overpowering. What we neglect in our attempts to live a carefully controlled existence is that the purpose of these behaviors is to preserve life, to awaken us to threats in our midst, and to call attention to what helps us survive.

While we are focusing on the embodied aspects here, it is important to remember that this project attempts to value the meaning of many of our fears differently. That is, if there is nothing to hope for, nothing that calls us into claiming and reclaiming the goodness of life, then we are destined to little more than raging and railing against a world that will do nothing but disappoint us with a constant barrage of threats and traumatic experiences. Furthermore, there is little reason to react to threats if there is no forward visioning of a better life. We do not survive just to survive; we survive, through the emotion of fear, with the hope of thriving and reclaiming a sense of the relational goodness of life. Thus it is important to mark the times in our lives when these behaviors arise, or when we feel the presence of a threat. While these times may be disruptive and/or destructive, they also provide a possible moment of contrast to the goodness of life that we subscribe to when calling ourselves persons of faith. In exploring these moments of contrast we can begin to see and author stories of hope that continue before, during, and after our experiences with a threat.

Turning back to these adaptable behavioral responses to threats we can put the final piece of the puzzle together related to the embodied emotion of fear. Looking at the purpose and conservation of these behaviors throughout our human history, Joseph LeDoux remarks that defensive behaviors "represent the operation of brain systems that have been programmed by evolution to deal with danger in routine ways."[6] While there may be some conscious control of the intensity of our reactions, there are also some constants when it comes to the behaviors associated with fear. Moreover, these patterns of behavior seem to have some consistency between human and nonhuman species.[7] Knowing that these behaviors exist in some shape or form in other species leads me to wonder if this is one of the reasons we tend to denigrate the emotion of fear theologically. To be like other species is to admit that we are in some small way not as special as we once thought. To give in to basic evolutionary protective measures is to admit that we are sometimes powerless and helpless in the face of threats or traumatic moments. Admitting this is difficult since our theology often seeks to prop humanity up as the pinnacle and crowning achievement of God's creative works. However, if our theology reflects a horizontal rather than hierarchical understanding of power and creativity, then seeing these parallels allows us a good bit of freedom to accept these behaviors as worthwhile, and honor their place in our lives.

Think for a moment about a time when you have been frightened. Reflect back on the moment you realized a threat was present. What was the first thing that happened? Most likely you froze. The brain kicks into high gear when the presence of a threat is noted. We tend to become hyper-attentive to the object of our fears; our pupils dilate, and much of our peripheral vision is banished. Now there are two types of freezing that can occur around a threat. The first is attentive freezing, where we attempt to hide from a threat while keeping a constant awareness of the position of the threat in our midst. The second form of freezing is called tonic immobility. Tonic immobility is described by Isaac Marks, a psychiatrist who has spent much of his life studying defensive behaviors, as "an extreme fear reaction in which the animal or person is 'scared stiff' and unresponsive to even painful or other intense stimulation."[8] Marks described tonic immobility as arising in situations such as rape, war, and attacks by wild animals. In these overwhelming situations we remain conscious, but we are somehow protecting important parts of ourselves from harm. Moreover, when we recover from this frozen state, often there is a burst of vigorous activity as we fight or flee. In most situations, our moment of frozen awareness is about preparing us to act upon the threat with one of the three remaining behaviors.

From freezing we move into two of the more familiar adaptive behaviors associated with fear: flight and fight. Between humans and nonhuman organisms, flight is probably the most utilized behavior associated with fear. As humans, we view our world through complex systems of interpretation, memories, and meaning. Thus we have developed a wide range of methods to withdraw from threats. We create new physical pathways that allow us to circumnavigate remembered places or objects; we withdraw internally from threats, shielding ourselves from damage when physical escape is not possible; as a mechanism to relieve the discomfort of the emotion of fear, we avoid discussing or engaging a remembered threat. We adopt new methods in order to mitigate feeling afraid because sometimes the best way to survive is not to put oneself in the path of dangerous objects. However, sometimes dangerous objects can't be avoided.

This leads us to the third behavior, which I believe is becoming more culturally prevalent today: fighting. The difference between this behavior and that of pure aggressiveness is that the goal is to escape. In humans, when a threat becomes real and escape is not immediately possible, we often resort to standing tall. We increase our physical outline or stare down an opponent in the hopes they back off; we may also search our immediate area for a weapon in order to change the dynamic of the situation. As Marks notes, "Bluff has always been a common human strategy to ward off attack, and disguise to elude capture."9

We can often see this in the moments of indignation that arise when strongly held beliefs are threatened. The rhetoric gets ratcheted up and our words grow stronger, with the intent that those who threaten our position will back down. What I think has happened today is that both conversation partners feel afraid and therefore demonize the position of the other. As these boastful bluffs continue, it becomes harder and harder to take another position, or even change our minds, collaborate, or compromise. Rather than escape, which is the goal of this behavior, the rhetoric rises and grows more extreme until people are in positions where their initial bluff becomes the baseline for beginning subsequent conversations. This kind of endless cycle ensures that we remain afraid of others and their particular positions, seeing them as threats.

The final defensive behavior associated with fear is less well known but certainly worth some attention. Two fairly distinctive behaviors fall under the category of appeasement—deflection and submission. Deflection refers to sacrificing a piece of ourselves to save what is vital. Humans might position themselves in a fight to receive blows on their arms and legs rather than vital organs; a parent might step between a child and a threat; in order to protect our sense of self, we might deflect certain topics of discussion or make a self-deprecating joke. Submission, as a form of appeasement, means standing small rather than tall. We shrink our presence and submit to the threat with the hope that our behavior will reduce the impact of that threat on our lives.

If we look at the structures of the brain and the well-honed behaviors that accompany the emotion of fear, we can begin to see just how inescapable it is. To summarize, the amygdala is the bundle of interconnected neurons most responsible for the emotion of fear. It is primarily connected to regions of our brain that receive sensory input, control our autonomic systems, and access our memories. When a threat or trauma arises, our brain kicks into gear; it uses the fast path between the thalamus and amygdala to release hormones that prepare us for action. Simultaneously, the slow pathway searches our memories for similar experiences or other moments when we felt afraid. Even while our body is preparing to react, a combination of memories, beliefs, and imaginings mitigate or reinforce certain behaviors. When a reaction of fear is called for, humans will most often behave by fighting, fleeing, freezing, or appeasing a threat. These embodied aspects of fear comprise what I understand to be its most inescapable aspects. To be afraid is a normal human reaction; the ways in which we culturally and theologically demonize fear is unnatural. Furthermore, our inability to embrace the role of fear in our lives has a detrimental impact on our ability to relate to others in meaningful and loving ways.

Embedded Fears: Memories, Beliefs, and Imagination

There is fear, and there are fears. The neurophysiological concepts we just examined point to the embodied emotion of fear; however, there are a multitude of objects that we fear. We now move to the embedded, or subjective, notion of fear. Human subjectivity is comprised of the interplay between memories, beliefs, imagination, emotions, and the ways in which we act upon these things in relation to our experiences of the world. The question of how we come to see an object as something to fear is the subject of the rest of this chapter. Fear is a relational emotion, and it often takes an experience with an object (or even a secondhand experience with something) to create a fear-based relationship. The objects we fear are coded into our brains as memories.

As we continue to have experiences with these objects, we develop beliefs about them by taking risks and filling in the gaps where our memory is incomplete. Furthermore, fear is an imaginative emotional state. The beliefs we develop about the things that threaten us often include a healthy dose of imaginative risk, and imagination plays a large part in the intensity of our reaction to threats.

Say we both have experiences with spiders that are tucked away in our memories. Out of these encounters we have developed a small fear of the creepy little creatures. Depending on the stories, and how much of our imagination we use relative to them, seeing a spider crawl down a wall will mean something different to each of us. Thus while you and I might both jump at the sight of a spider ambling across the floor, one of us might jump higher and farther depending on our interpretation of that spider as a threat. The same threat triggers reactions that vary in intensity based upon the memories, beliefs, and imaginings that go into our interpretation of that moment. Furthermore, the intensity of our emotional memories about spiders will guide the intensity of our reaction in that moment.

Interpreting an experience involves more than just the facts of what has, is, or will occur. When we interpret, we remember, we believe, and we imagine. As neuroscientist Alain Berthoz remarks,

> [m]aking a decision requires associating events, sensations, memories, and so on. This work of association is carried out in part in the amygdala. But making a decision also requires deliberating over it, changing one's point of view, mentally altering the relations between associated elements, and simulating different possible realities. So it has to be somewhat flexible.[10]

Not only do our interpretations call forth our memories, beliefs, and imaginative rumblings, they also incorporate feelings, actions, and reasoned responses. Given the interplay of all of these things, it is no wonder that we each can come up with unique stories and emotional reactions related to the same experience. A subjective fear is much more complex than just the neurophysiological reaction to an object..

MEMORY

Think for a moment about sharing an experience with someone. What information do you share? How do you describe the setting or set the tone for the story? Are you just relaying the facts as you see them, or are you adding an emotional layer as well? My guess is that an honest answer to these questions begins with "It depends . . ." We might share more with a family member than a stranger. With certain friends we might add an emotional lens to our stories. What we remember depends often upon the person who sparks the story. Each time we tell the same story, it is not the same story. Our memories and how we remember are not exact duplicates of experiences.[11] Each time we remember, we construct a new story about an object based on past experiences. Furthermore, emotions direct our attention to specific parts of a story, and our imagination often fills in the gaps where the knowledge we store is incomplete. Memory and remembering are fascinating topics, especially in the context of faith. However, for our purposes it is the intersection of memory and emotion that really helps us understand what we come to fear in life.

Memory is thought of as both a process and as stored knowledge. As a process, memory has to do with the encoding and retrieving of the things that have been stored in our neural pathways. Remember the amygdala? Neuroscientists have lately been exploring its relationship to memory. One of the current theories is that the amygdala plays a role in stamping memories with specific emotional content. In turn, these emotional memories are more vivid, last longer than other memories, and are easier to recall.[12] Think about these in the context of the emotion of fear; if we come in contact with a threat, our memory of that threat endures longer, is more vivid, and is easier to recall than other memories. This gives these memories a tremendous amount of power relative to how we interpret the world. As we continue, keep in mind that memory refers to a process of encoding, retrieval, and storage. Memory consists of both memories and the process of writing and retrieving them.

In the encoding phase, the emotion of fear narrows our field of vision as we focus in on a threat. This suggests that these emotional memories are a bit more narrowly focused and contain specific information about a threat. Often we become so focused on the threat that other stimuli fade into the background. Think for a moment about the impact this has on specific experiences. When we become focused on a threat, we often forget other skills, coping mechanisms, or even hopeful realizations. During this encoding phase, what becomes associated with that memory is fear and how we responded to the threat in that moment. What this means is that the emotion of fear adds an additional interpretive layer to an experience, so that during the retrieval phase of a memory we can more quickly assess a threat and respond.

These subjective interpretations may be most evident during the retrieval phase of the remembering process. Every new experience is interpreted through layers of themes or associations with past experiences. In every present moment, there are multitudes of past memories that ebb and flow as we interpret and react to what is happening. Some of these interpretive layers have emotional content and some don't. As we think about past fear-based experiences, the vivid nature of these memories often direct our attention to particular features of a new experience, even to the point that we might feel fear in what may be an otherwise neutral experience. So far, we have discussed the process of creating and remembering memories. However, it may be in the storage of fear-based memories that we see how our unique fears arise.

We are many things, but in many ways we are our memories. The knowledge we store related to experiences and their emotional and mental content forms the backbone of many of our interpretive lenses. Going back to the spider analogy, how high and how far you jump (assuming you move at all) because of a spider is based upon the cumulative knowledge and experiences you have had with spiders in the past. Our reaction is completely unique to our person. Humans use similar processes to encode, retrieve, and store memories, but how we interpret an object shapes what we choose to uniquely store about it. In turn, each day we store more and more unique knowledge, and that impacts the ways we interpret the world. As we continue to live, breathe, and become, we develop habits as stories are reinforced or challenged through new experiences. In this way, we are constantly forming new interpretive lenses through which we approach the world and our experiences. That said, some interpretations die hard, often based on how strong an emotional response is encoded with the experiences. Many of these habitual emotional memories live at the core of our beliefs.

BELIEFS

Beliefs are inherently risky assumptions and attitudes that we hold about particular persons, objects, groups, or concepts. As assumptions, beliefs are imperfect (much like our memories). As attitudes, beliefs inform our dispositions toward particular objects. Furthermore, beliefs require us to take a risk; they require us to use our imagination to draw a link between what we think and what we experience.[13] Beliefs are interesting inasmuch as they guide many of our actions in life. However, it is when we couple beliefs with emotions that we really understand their impact on our worlds.

Finish the sentence "I believe . . ." What were your first responses? You might have responded with something like "I believe in love" or "I believe in God." As you tend to those responses, take a step back and think about where they come from. You most likely pulled the remainder of that sentence from your memory. Taking that memory a step further, you may have learned something in school, church, or life that made those the first responses to this fill-in-the-blank. Now, if you answered with something this broad, you are taking a risk (even if you were more specific, there is risk in that as well). To say you believe in love or God is to risk taking an experience of something valuable and interpreting it as a meaningful lens through which the world makes sense. To believe in love is to agree to act in a certain way toward yourself and others. Thus when we describe a belief, we are taking a position on the world as it relates to us. Beliefs are the mental gymnastics we do to make sense of things that have happened to us throughout our life.

Personally, I believe that communities of faith, and indeed our faiths in general, are ultimately relational. This belief comes from being an awkward teenager who never felt like he fit in with most of the world. In my formative years, I viewed the church I attended as a safe relational space to try out different ideas about myself. I found more acceptance there than other places, and thus developed a belief that communities of faith should be first and foremost about relationship. Throughout the years, as I studied more and more about the church I was constantly interpreting what I learned through this relational lens. While this may sound like an intellectual pursuit, it is not. The importance of my belief about the relationships we should share and build in communities of faith has great emotional strength behind it. It stems from a feeling of belonging, care, and concern I sense that all communities of faith should share; additionally, some of its strength is derived from the anger I feel toward religious mouthpieces who continue to divide and deride others who are different. What we need to understand about beliefs is that they are more than just intellectual ideas. Beliefs shape our interactions with the world, and our emotions impact our beliefs in a variety of ways. This idea merits further exploration.

One group of psychologists propose that "emotions can awaken, intrude into, and shape beliefs, by creating them, by amplifying or altering them, and by making them resistant to change."[14] This is a complicated way of saying that emotions are intimately intertwined with our beliefs. They are so connected that when we experience a specific emotion, it impacts the beliefs we hold to be true. Experiencing love might challenge a belief that the world is isolating and lonely; experiencing fear might change a belief that the world is a safe place. Emotions might create a new belief, where none previously existed. Think about the 9/11 attacks. The emotion of fear we experienced awakened beliefs in many that the world is a dangerous place. In others, the fear awakened a belief that respect and pulling together as a global community was vital. As a result of these emotional states, new beliefs were born and were acted upon in the world. As a result of each of these emotionally charged beliefs, those who felt a palpable fear started a war, and those who needed connection held numerous benefit concerts and worship services.

Emotions enhance and intensify our beliefs. I imagine this is why it is so easy for partisan ideas to flourish. When a belief we hold true is challenged, we fear another's position that runs counter to our own. Psychologists Gerald Clore and Karen Gasper propose that "[a]n increase in emotional intensity may further narrow attentional focus, making relevant events seem even more important, leading to still greater intensity, and so on in an ever-narrowing circle."[15] Let's say someone believes that their church is dying. They might feel emotions like fear, shame, guilt, and/or anger. As a result of these emotions, the belief in the death of a church intensifies and the person takes on a position of life at all costs. Thus they scrutinize the worship attendance; they intensely critique a pastor's sermons or the way they do their job; they might even reject new ideas in order to conserve the church the way it is. The intensity of the belief cuts off the ability to focus on new possibilities, which effectively narrows the scope of a person's ability to act contrary to a particular belief.

Emotions play a significant role in shaping the beliefs we use to interpret and interact with our worlds. Emotions can sometimes awaken beliefs, intrude into and intensify them, and even create new ones. Thinking about the role of memory and emotions in all of this, when an experience and the emotion of fear interact, there is a distinct possibility that an enduring belief will form. Fear-tinged beliefs, developed out of the memories of experiences, inform how we respond to new situations. Ultimately, emotions, memories, and beliefs impact our ability to imagine and empathize with the world around us.

IMAGINATION

With each new experience, we interpret, we remember, and we engage our imaginations. We draw connections between our beliefs and what is unfolding before our eyes, and creatively put all the pieces together to make sense of what is happening. To imagine is to utilize our creative capacities to construct novel ideas, concepts, or stories from fragments of our memory-shaped beliefs about the world. The greatest limitations to our imaginations are the breadth of our knowledge about the world and the creative capacities we are willing to put into practice to understand and create new stories. Imagination is a source of pleasure and pain; it can help us concoct possibilities, but it can also create hostility and isolation. As pastoral theologian David Hogue states, "Imagination is not merely a source of pleasure. The creations of our minds can frighten as well as inspire and comfort us."[16]

Understanding imagination requires us to see it as the capacity to dream and hope, as well as the capacity to dread. The emotion of fear can play a large role in coloring the future for us. Often seen and experienced in the negative, fear can be a source of the dreadful possibilities we invent in the dark of night. The ability to predict the future based on our imaginations is "a two-edged sword . . . if what we see is dark and foreboding, we become weighed down with inaction and despair."[17] Our imagination is vital to any experience of hope; at the same time, it can play a vital role in coloring our future with dread. If all we can imagine is the feeling of fear in an imagined experience, then chances are we will avoid that kind of experience or react negatively should the experience find us.

For all of the negatives I am pointing to here, we must remember that our imagination is the source of all that could be, and what could be is also a source of great hope and possibility. When we imagine, we construct a future by putting together the pieces of our memories in new ways.

Think about the old hymn "Onward Christian Soldiers." Now, put that song and its militaristic language in the context of the phrase "God is love." How does one impact the other? How does it draw out specific language that reinterprets it? Depending on your experiences with both phrases, you could put together the meaning of these two phrases in more ways than can be counted. You can interpret the song through the lens of love and what that means; you can reject the song and its content based on love; you can redefine love based on the content of the song; or, you can bring in a multitude of other experiences to further complicate the interpretation and imagined meanings. Our imaginations can re-create, rationalize, and/or redefine the relationship between these two seemingly different ideas.

CONCLUSION

I can imagine feeling a little overwhelmed by all of this information; I can also imagine feeling a bit perplexed as to how this helps us redeem the emotion of fear. Looking at it from this point of view seems to further affirm the need for not being afraid, as scripture tells us. However, let's carry those imaginative thoughts into a personal faith journey. Imagine being told all your life that fear is a weakness; that those with true faith do not fear what the world brings into their lives. Now, imagine having your world shaken by an overwhelming experience of fear—a trauma, a threat, or a natural disaster. How would you feel in those moments? How would you redefine your faith through the lenses of these new experiences? Imagine the freedom we might experience to explore new possibilities and interpretations if we were told that fear is a normal and natural part of our existence. If we are freed from the shame of being afraid, how might we experience those emotional memories in new and novel ways? What if our communities of faith took seriously what we are learning about the brain and humanity? How might we become the houses of hope that we claim to be? I am of the mind that we can only transform that which we are willing to acknowledge; we can only deal with that which we recognize in our midst. Fear surrounds us in this day and age; the more we ignore it with simple platitudes, the more it grows and envelops our communities and lives.

For all the data in this chapter that may point to the contrary, I still believe that fear is a gift; it is part of the relational and imaginative structures of our lives. Fear is embodied; and, fears are embedded into the fabric of our lives. That we will experience fear is an inescapable reality. Yet, how we choose to deal with our fears in the future is a great source of imaginative possibility.

QUESTIONS FOR REFLECTION

1. In Chapter 1, we briefly discussed the *Imago Dei*. Based on those words and what we know about the brain, how does this shift your thinking about what it means to be made in the image of God?
2. Furthermore, based on our physical presence in the world, how do you understand the idea of embodiment and the *Imago Dei*?
3. Do you buy the argument that fear is inescapable? If so, what does that mean about our relationship with God and the world? If not, how do you reconcile what we are learning about the human brain and a theological understanding of humanity?
4. Using your imagination, think about the necessity of the emotion of fear. What reason would God have for creating this capacity within us?
5. Think about your particular community of faith for a moment. How do you see stories colored with the emotion of fear in your own midst? How do you acknowledge or ignore them?

Notes

1. Luke Johnson and Joseph LeDoux, "The Anatomy of Fear: Microcircuits of the Lateral Amygdala," in *Fear & Anxiety: The Benefits of Translational Research*, ed. J. M. Gorman (Washington, DC: American Psychiatric Publishing, 2004), 228.
2. Stefan Linquist, "Prospects for a Dual Inheritance Model of Emotional Evolution," *Philosophy of Science* 74, (2007): 849.
3. I take a process view of evolution that begins with the idea that God creates out of chaos and goes something like this . . . Evolution is the best theoretical framework for understanding the origins of humanity, with the most evidence to support it. As a theologian, I take the view that

God works in history through the evolutionary process to bring us to this point in time. Human evolution, as I understand it, is a series of genetic mutations that are selected for over the course of human history. Especially early on in the formation of life, process theology would posit that co-determinative events happened. That is, God worked in relationship with organisms to effect change. The response to God's lure in these creative moments brought about novel evolutionary leaps, sometimes to the benefit of the world, sometimes not. These co-determinative moments rarely reach the pinnacle of God's intent. I believe this can open us up to a lot of possibilities. On a more positive note, it allows us to incorporate a wider sense of what science is teaching us about the world and humanity. Furthermore, it reminds us of God's intimate involvement in the world. Of course the flip side is that humans, in their current state, are pale imitations of our co-determinative relationship with God. We were intended to be so much more, but in fact aren't. Thus evolution is both a progressive and a failing enterprise.

4. Joseph LeDoux, "Fear and the Brain: Where Have We Been, and Where Are We Going?," *Biological Psychiatry* 44, no. 12 (1998): 1229.

5. These two pathways are called the thalmo-amygdala (fast) and thalmo-cortico-amygdala (slow). You can think about these as the difference between an interstate and a highway. Both allow for quick processing, but the interstate will get you to your destination sooner. The difference in processing between these two pathways is in the milliseconds.

6. Joseph LeDoux, *The Emotional Brain: The Mysterious Underpinnings of Emotional Life* (New York: Simon & Schuster Paperbacks, 1996), 128.

7. This overlap between some structures of the brain and their associated behaviors gave rise to the idea of the "lizard brain," often described as the most primitive of the brain structures, as in the triune brain theory developed by Paul MacLean (see *The Triune Brain in Evolution* [New York: Plenum, 1989]), who described three distinct evolutionary formations within the structures of the brain. Each interconnected structure has discrete functions and intelligences that delineate its role and purpose, but also distinguish its level of complexity. The problem with this point of view is that while there are interconnected centers of activity in the brain, these centers are vastly more complex and not easily distinguishable into distinct regions that exist for solely one purpose.

8. Isaac Marks, *Fears, Phobias, and Rituals: Panic, Anxiety, and Their Disorders* (Oxford: Oxford University Press, 1987), 60–61.

9. Ibid., 72.

10. Alain Berthoz, *Emotion and Reason: The Cognitive Neuroscience of Decision Making*, trans. Giselle Weiss (Oxford: Oxford University Press, 2006), 203.

11. Memory is a term that means different things to different groups of people. The study of memory is a multidisciplinary task. Moreover, there has been some difficulty agreeing on what the term means. On a conceptual level, psychologist Schacter remarks that memory refers to "the neurocognitive capacity to encode, store and retrieve information" (Daniel Schacter, "Memory: Delineating the Core," in *Science of Memory: Concepts,* ed. H. Roediger III et al. [Oxford: Oxford University Press, 2007], 26). I tend to agree with this conceptual model or memory, despite its reliance on completely functional language. When you attempt to broaden a definition of memory beyond this concept, things become much more complex. We could talk about short- and long-term memory, episodic, involuntary, or voluntary memories. I am intentionally not going to engage these branches of memory study, despite my respect for them. However, if you wish to explore memory on a conceptual level, there are works by Tulving, Schacter, and Mace that I have found helpful.

12. See Larry Cahill, "Modulation of Long-Term Memory Storage in Humans by Emotional Arousal: Adrenergic Activation and the Amygdala," in *The Amygdala: A Functional Analysis*, ed. John Aggleton (Oxford: Oxford University Press, 2000), 425–45; and Bryan Strange and Raymond Dolan, "Anterior Medial Temporal Lobe in Human Cognition: Memory for Fear and the Unexpected," *Cognitive Neuropsychiatry* 11, no. 3 (2006): 198–218. for more information about emotions and memories.

13. Psychologists Nico Frijda, Antony Manstead, and Sacha Bem remark that "[b]eliefs can be defined as states that link a person or group or object or concept with one or more attributes, and this is held by the believer to be true" ("The Influence of Emotions on Beliefs," in *Emotions and Beliefs: How Feelings Influence Thoughts,* ed. Nico Frijda et al. [Cambridge: Cambridge University Press, 2000], p. 5).

14. Frijda, Manstead, and Bem, 2000, 122.

15. Gerald Clore and Karen Gasper, "Feeling Is Believing: Some Affective Influences on Belief," in *Emotions and Beliefs: How Feelings Influence Thoughts*, ed. Nico Frijda et al. (Cambridge: Cambridge University Press, 2000), 11.

16. David Hogue, *Remembering the Future, Imagining the Past: Story, Ritual, and the Human Brain* (Cleveland: Pilgrim, 2003), 15.

17. Anthony Reading, *Hope & Despair: How Perceptions of the Future Shape Human Behavior* (Baltimore: Johns Hopkins University Press, 2004), 127.

4

Communities of Faith, Communities of Fear

Emotions intrude into and embellish the fabric of our culture and communities; they shape the ways we remember certain experiences; they form part of the backbone of the risks we take in interpreting and believing certain things about the world. Emotions are also part of the imaginative framework through which we project our expectations of the future. Mention the simple phrase "9/11" in the United States and most citizens alive during that time will recall both facts and emotions. Many will give you details, but most will remember how they felt as well. They might project auras of fear, sorrow, disgust, anger, or frustration.

In the current political environment, emotions are utilized and manipulated to develop arguments about particular positions. Political positions are built upon emotionally charged beliefs; these usually take on a destructive position relative to another person, rather than a constructive position about an issue. This not only calls into question how we utilize emotions to create beliefs and project a worldview into the future, but more so how emotions are intertwined in our communities and social gatherings.

If emotions pervade the stories we tell, if they focus our attention on specific details, if they make certain experiences easier to recall and last longer, then how do emotions impact and shape the structure of our lives together? In particular, how does the emotion of fear shape our relationships with one another and the experiences we share in this world?

In an earlier chapter, we discussed the rise of a culture of fear that pervades the fabric of American life. I attributed this to the rise in availability of vicarious traumas and threats accessible through media outlets. This is not to say that the media are solely to blame for our culture of fear; that is simply too easy. Our ability to interpret, reflect, and relay the stories we learn and/or experience plays a role in the propagation of fear in our culture.

Rather, the constant awareness of possible threats creates a need to feel hypervigilant about our surroundings. That hypervigilance is born in how we relate to one another; in whether we risk conversation with a stranger; in whether we demonize a culture, issue, or population; in how we understand faith and choose to live it out in an often broken and fearful world. When we are aware of threats, when they dominate the landscape or give rise to personal stories of fear, it impacts how we talk, care, love, and relate to one another.

Think for a moment about what you choose to watch on television, or if you have forsaken that medium, where you choose to get your news. What are the headlines that grab your attention? How do these sources of knowledge choose to portray specific situations? As political scientist Leonie Huddy remarks,

> politicians and the media frequently contribute to such fear mongering by portraying an isolated incident as a trend, which is often designed to deflect attention away from more dangerous but politically unpalatable situations. The pervasive political practice of consciously arousing public fears through the presentation of frightening statistics is doubly disturbing when coupled with the tendency of anxious people to overestimate risk.[1]

Take a moment to remember the news stories that you watch and read. How were emotional appeals used in order to draw you into that story? How did they use language to convey particular information and define the actors in that story? Moreover, how did that story distract you from something or someone more pertinent, pressing, or meaningful? Not only do we get a reporting of the facts, but every story is layered with interpretations of the events. From how the headline is shaped to the copy on the teleprompter, words are carefully examined and chosen to convey a particular emotional experience related to a story. This not only shapes our hearing of the story, but also shapes how we tell that same story to others.

This is not just limited to the news media. Think about the popular religious television voices for a moment. Some of them use a bully pulpit to express their fears of change. They spend much of their time condemning the world with language steeped in judgment and wrath. Other television preachers fear being irrelevant and therefore espouse extreme positions that ensure their place in the limelight for just a little while longer. Some present a position so saccharine that it cannot deal with the hostility and injustice of the world in meaningful ways. All of these emotional appeals can be used to manipulate someone's faith; and we carry these emotions into our communities in very meaningful and tangible ways.

Fear, as a tool of manipulation, becomes a useful way to hold our attention. When we accept someone else's fearful interpretation of an event, it narrows our focus. Living in fear keeps us from taking a broader view of the world. The manipulation of our capacity to experience fear can keep us from being flexible about the changes we experience in the world, hardening specific positions, beliefs, and ideals.

Fear, as it is abused by powerful voices in our culture, keeps us placated, frozen, and dependent on others. Most often, those who perpetuate these stories are quick to offer remedies to make us feel safe again. Fear-based rhetoric is intended to make us feel powerless and helpless; it is an attempt to ensure our dependence on someone or something by narrowing our choices and limiting our imagination. As one political scientist warns us, "There is a broad tendency for threatened individuals to become less tolerant of difference, leading in turn to an increased reliance on stereotypes and a heightened animosity toward outsiders."[2] Look for a moment at your own life, the news you consume, the pundits you frequently read and quote. Liberal or progressive, libertarian or republican, how do they speak about the events of the world? Moreover, how do they interpret the way others speak of the world? Do they leave room for the possibility that there are multiple ways of interpreting events, or do they only see one solution? Are they capable of listening to alternative views and finding value in the differences, or when they encounter an alternative do they merely grow louder and more obstinate?

While it is important to understand these sources of our fear, we bear responsibility for how they are incorporated into our lives. Indeed, the most important question in this search for the sources of our societal fears may be how we accept and incorporate certain narratives into our lives. When you hear a pundit spout absolutes, whether progressive or conservative, how much of that message do you internalize? How much of their story becomes your story? How much of their fundamentalism becomes paramount to your fundamental safety?

Remember, fear is relational. However, the emotion of fear is often concerned with how we might end a relationship with a particular threat. The more things we come to see as threats in our lives, the more our relationships narrow. When we are afraid, our first impulse is to alleviate the emotional toll it takes on our lives; therefore, we often endeavor to end a relationship with an object that we feel threatens us. At the same time, I contend that as we end one relationship we also try to establish relationships with those things we view as secure and stable; we attempt to find something that we can connect to in order to reclaim a semblance of the goodness of life. These individual pursuits of safety affect the relational fabric in which we live and move and become.

Our individual world is unalterably intertwined with our social and relational realities. Fear can be like a virus, shared from one person to the next. Thus when we act out of a sense of hypervigilance that separates us from one another, we end up sharing some of the fear we are experiencing. A culture of fear is not just a personal experience of communal stories; it is something that shapes our relationships with one another. A culture of fear can create communities that live in fear of the world around them.

We are social creatures, we are curious, we are imaginative, and we are interactive. Fear can play into each of these benefits of being human; at the same time these things also imply that we are hopeful creatures as well. Thus while fear enables us to run from certain things, I believe it also orients us so that we are running toward something life-giving as well.

As we continue to explore how fear is transmitted socially, and how it impacts our cultures and communities, we must be willing to entertain the idea that these stories of threat and trauma include meaningful threads of hope. I firmly believe that when we experience the emotion of fear, hope is also present—that implicit in many of these stories are strands of hope begging to be recognized. However, these hopes only becomes real as we reflect on our stories and how they might reveal moments of resistance and resilience that point to a desire to survive, cope, and thrive.

THE SOCIAL SHARING OF FEAR

Let's remember that when it comes to fear, there are two different ways of discussing its impact. The first is through the neural mechanisms that make the emotion of fear inescapable; the second is the conditioned or learned aspects of fear that come about through our experiences. We have talked a bit about what it means to personally experience fear and how the brain processes the emotion. We've also discussed how we learn to be afraid through particular experiences we have in the world. In this chapter, we are expanding this idea to think about fear on a communal level. That is, fear can be expressed and transmitted from person to person in ways that create shared narratives based on threats and traumas.

As someone who enjoys hiking, I generally look forward with great anticipation to times when I can strap on my boots and hit a new trail. I look forward to seeing new surroundings, to testing myself and my abilities, to getting outdoors and experiencing nature firsthand. Let's say my spouse and I decide to try a new trail in an unfamiliar area. We do our research and know that there have been previous sightings of mountain goats, bighorn sheep, and even mountain lions in the area. None of these are especially frightening to us, as the sightings are rare and animals generally avoid human contact if possible. Hiking, in general, is a positive experience and we look forward to getting out as soon as possible.

As we are moving along, about a mile up the trail we see a group of hikers on their way back to the trailhead. They are moving fairly quickly, but there is nothing immediately alarming about this. However, as we round a switchback, we see more clearly their frantic pace. As they near us, we notice that their eyes are wide open, and they seem out of breath. We can feel some of the tension they are experiencing ooze off of them. Their faces are pale and they are so focused on the trail in front of them they are startled by our presence. As they draw near, one of them breathily states, "If you are going to keep going, be really careful." Without another word, they pass right by and continue on their way. We look at each other and try and reflect on what we just saw and heard. Deciding to continue on our way, we are vigilant in scanning our surroundings, and our hearts pound a little harder in our chests.

Fear-based narratives are not only shared person-to-person, they also can take on a life of their own in a group. For example, the annual congregational meeting at your community of faith is generally uneventful; information about the church, its programs, its finances, and its plans are shared. This year begins the same as every other; however, you know that in a moment you have to give a report on the church's budget deficit and its net loss of members over the course of the year. As the meeting starts, things seem to be going well, until you reach these two reports. At that time, a longtime and well-respected member of your faith community stands angrily and begins to speak out about the loss of members and revenue. It seems he came prepared, as he quotes articles about the declining membership in mainline denominations. He talks about this year in the red as being the first of many if the community doesn't change its ways. He sees the decline in membership as indicative of poor pastoral leadership, a hostile culture and community, and he ends with several dire warnings about the future.

As you look out upon the gathered community of faith, you see a mix of facial expressions and body language. Some seem to resonate with what he is saying; their faces contort with anger and sadness. Others seem to have disconnected, their eyes wandering around the room. When he sits down, others begin to rise and express their frustrations; they look at the events of the past year, the people they lost to other churches, to death, and to the movement of life, and they express their fears about this being the beginning of a death spiral for the church. Some rise to call for a greater push in evangelism; some believe that the community needs to draw closer to support one another against this threat to their survival; still others see this as the first warning shot about the need to fight for the survival of the church against cultural pressures. The meeting continues to devolve into a series of rants and opinions that have little to do with the community of faith, and more to do with opinions and nightmares about the future.

For a moment, reflect on where your own imagination took you in response to those stories. How did you react? Were you curious about what lay ahead? In the first story, did you find yourself wanting to tell the two of us to turn around and go home? In the second story, how did you react to hearing the negative interpretations of the information? What were your physical/emotional/mental reactions to the stories? Think about your own experiences. What did these stories recall for you? Furthermore, how did those experiences inform the way you responded to each story? Finally, how did your imagination fill in the gaps of each story to make it more suspenseful and frightening, or even try and diffuse the emotional impact it might have?

Research from neuropsychologists sheds a little light into what is happening in these stories. In the first story, we experienced the emotion of fear through engaging our imaginations around the facial expressions, bodily movements, tone, and words of the people who passed us on the trail. As a result, we become more vigilant about our surroundings, allowing our imaginations to fill in the details that were not shared with us. Neuropsychologists Andreas Olsson and Elizabeth Phelps believe that we can become afraid merely by watching someone react to a threat or by being told we should be afraid. They think that this ability to transmit fear has its roots in our evolution, providing a significant advantage over others who could not process these same facial expressions and social cues.[3] They see this ability to read and experience the emotions of another (also called the ability to empathize) as a practical adaptation to the world around us. Learning vicariously through others' experiences gives us a better shot at recognizing and dealing with the impact of threats more quickly.

These same two neuropsychologists examine the role that language plays in the transmission of fear. The tone and use of specific language in the stories we tell convey an emotional experience to others. We see this happening in the community of faith example, where one interpretation of information breeds a host of emotional responses in line with the experience of fear. As Olsson and Phelps remark, "Language forces the receiver to rely on similar past experiences and internally generated imagery to establish an emotional memory."[4] When we hear a significant emotional story, we tend to jump into our memories and search for a comparable experience. Numerous associations can be made around the content of a story, the emotions it exudes, or even words or phrases that trigger our own memories and experiences. Coupled with a healthy imagination, these stories take on a new life as we imagine scenarios and possibilities lurking around the corner.

In certain social situations, we might consider the emotion of fear to behave like a virus. It infects not only the original source, but can also be passed from person to person with a simple look, the invocation of a phrase, or a specific tone of voice. When we get certain cues from others, it recalls personal experiences that run parallel to what is happening before us. Even though these memories may have nothing to do with that current experience, there is some relationship between the two. In the space between what we know and what we are experiencing, our imaginations and rooted beliefs fill in the blanks. Our imagination can be a terrible, wonderful, and powerful thing; it is a gap-filler, allowing us to live out different possibilities in our mind's eye. In the same way that we use our imaginations to create worlds of amazing fantasy, we also use it in ways that cause our worlds to evolve into something much worse. Imagination plays an important role by directing the attention of the human mind in present and future moments based on the knowledge contained in the memories of our past. What we imagine is the result of memories rearranged and reconstructed creatively in order to provide a new way to interpret present and future experiences. With a minimal dose of imagination, the relational aspects of fear expand beyond the boundaries of our minds and infect the world around us. Likewise, it is our imaginations that help us see and project hopeful realities into the world around us as well.

A Case Study in Communal Fear

Turning to a case study for a moment, imagine that you are called in to help a struggling congregation. As you read the case study, think about the variety of communities you attend to in your life. Replay in your mind the rhetoric and values displayed in their activities together. As you hear the stories about Calvary Church, hear the stories of your own communities, be they houses of worship, community organizations, families, or political groups. Imagine, if you will, being sent to Calvary Church as a consultant, and below are the things you observe.

The members of Calvary Church believe it is dying. Each Sunday, week after week, year after year, they gather in the morning and the worship space seems to grow larger. Most of the remaining membership is comprised of loyal founders of the church. They grew up in this community, and will often talk about the glory days of humble, but rapid, growth in the beginning. When you ask members about what excites them today, they remain mostly silent. They point to relationships with people they have known for a long time as the glue that keeps them together; any excitement about the community is directed toward programs and studies that ended years ago.

Many of the members seem tired or resigned, although some are angry. They point suspiciously to the surrounding culture and changing community as the reasons for their isolation and dwindling numbers. They claim indignantly that the younger generation doesn't show them or their church the respect it deserves; they point fingers at the community around them, now mostly Hispanic, and talk about how these people don't understand the church. And yet, when you talk to people in the community, no one seems to know much about the church. Those who used to volunteer now claim they are too tired and don't have the energy to help any longer. Some are desperate to find new blood and life to inject into the church community; others, it seems, are content to let it dwindle and die, resigned to the idea that nothing they do will change the result.

Calvary Church exhibits many of the characteristics of a community locked into a set of fearful narratives. They are overwhelmed by the threat of their demise. Some of them, simply too tired to fight or flee, appease the threat by simply waiting for the church to die. They turn inward in order to protect what is left. Others are angry. Some direct this anger outward and attempt to fight or vilify the forces they see as threats; some use their anger to feed their suspicion about the populations that surround them. Together, they stand taller and develop a story filled with hostile rhetoric toward those they believe threaten them. They eye the world with a hostile suspicion that pushes new people away and feeds their fears of being misunderstood. Their hostility and resignation narrows their ability to connect with others outside of their community. They find safety and security within the walls of the church, and with the dwindling community that resides there.

As you delve deeper into the stories they share, you find out a couple of things about the church. First, what Calvary does well is care for one another. They know each other; they call when someone is missing from church; they show up when someone dies, or when one of their families is in need; they celebrate and remember one another's milestones. Despite their stories of exhaustion and resignation, when the need arises they live into stories of deep care for one another. Furthermore, there are stories in their history about reaching out to the community around them. The members felt value in contributing to nonprofits in their community and the mission work of their denomination. They stopped doing this when money became tight and when community organizations moved or closed their doors. Every once in a while they will have a special offering for a missionary or a group in the community, but this is the extent of their involvement as a church. The odd thing you notice is that even those who don't seem overwhelmed by the community's fears are paralyzed. They want to move, to do something different, to live, and yet they do nothing. While they haven't internalized many of the fearful narratives, they are impacted by the others and their fear and despair.

Coming into a community of faith that is gripped by fearful narratives can be exhausting and frustrating; remember, fear has tangible physical effects on us. My hypothesis about the effects of fear includes the idea that once we accept a certain level of fear in our lives and stories, it creates a new baseline for us. Thus we may be more sensitive to stories that corroborate our ideas about the world. A family that visits the church and doesn't return feeds suspicions that a younger generation doesn't value the church. A business moving from the neighborhood to another location becomes a statement about the community as a whole. As we become more sensitive and vigilant toward the world around us, we make interpretive leaps that often don't match up with the facts. Instead of seeking a better understanding, we feed a belief system built upon the fears we have cultivated and embodied in the stories of our lives.

The folks at Calvary may be right. Their church may be dying, and indeed there may be a time when its doors will close. However, looking at the complete anthology of stories they tell, there may be more going on at Calvary than just their fearful narratives. With each story we tell in life, there are multiple facets of that experience that go untold. For every suspicion about a business closing its doors, there is an offering taken for a missionary; for every family that visits and doesn't return, there is an outpouring of support for families in the fold who experience death or trauma in their lives. Remember, fear narrows our vision and focuses our attention. Broadening these stories is one of the primary goals of helping those gripped by a bevy of fear-based narratives. Our lives reflect complexity, and the stories we tell and share should reflect this idea. If we are to have hope, we cannot abide in simple explanations alone. We must, as listeners and speakers, begin to see how people are actively resisting and displaying resilience in the face of their fear-based narratives.

As you continue to read, put together a plan for engaging the community at Calvary Church. We will come back to this narrative later in the book, but this is a good time for you to explore how you might experience a community of faith in this situation. You might even look to the experiences you share in community with others and wonder how fearful narratives have crept into the life of those relationships. Two sets of questions are offered below; one set pertains to the case study, while the other continues to explore some of our personal attitudes toward fear and hope.

QUESTIONS FOR REFLECTION

CASE STUDY REFLECTIONS

1. If you were called into Calvary Church, what questions would you ask of them?
2. How might you approach their suspicions on a theological, practical, and personal level?
3. How might you deal with your own exhaustion and frustration without internalizing the stories of the community?
4. The practices of caregivers in pastoral situations are most often centered on hope, and the reclamation of the goodness of life in the midst of challenging circumstances. How might you help the community without completely denying the stories of fear they carry with them?
5. Finally, what if you were a member at Calvary? If you were immersed in these stories, how might you take a step back and reflect on their impact on the community of faith, and indeed the community as a whole?
6. How might you both acknowledge the reality of the situation and the fear it spawns, while at the same time pointing out the possibilities of living differently?

GENERAL QUESTIONS FOR REFLECTION

1. As we begin to make an explicit turn toward examining fear from a theological perspective, what hang-ups about this important emotion keep you from embracing its adaptive qualities?
2. Look at your own life for a moment. What are the fear-based narratives that seem to dominate your landscape of interpretation? What stories about culture, life, people, places, or politics do you buy without reflection?
3. As we pull together the social and neuropsychological science research presented so far, how do you understand the role that fear plays in our lives and our communities?

4. Furthermore, what possibilities for adaptation, survival, coping, and thriving do you see in these stories and experiences?

Notes

1. Leonie Huddy, "Fear and How It Works: Science and the Social Sciences," *Social Research* 71, no. 4 (2004): 803.

2. Ibid., 802.

3. Andreas Olsson and Elizabeth Phelps, "Social Learning of Fear," *Nature Neuroscience* 10, no. 9 (2007): 1096.

4. Ibid., 1099.

PART 3

A Pastoral Theology of Fear and Hope

In part 3, we will take an explicit theological turn as we continue to probe the usefulness of fear for the faithful. Up to now, we have been applying a lot of social and neuropsychological research to understand what it means to be afraid and how fear affects our lives and communities. Over the next three chapters we will shift to the development of a theological understanding of the emotion of fear and its relationship to hope.

Chapter 5 introduces some of the ideas found in process theology. I find process theology provides some helpful ways to conceive of God and our relationship to God. Through this brief introduction to process theology we will examine the concept of relational power, as well as explore how ideas of freedom and God's immanence can shape our understanding of fear.

Turning to the chapter 6, we will begin to draw out the connection between fear and hope as intertwined in many experiences of threat and trauma. Much of my understanding of hope is shaped around experiences of resistance and resilience in the face of threatening experiences.

5

A Process Perspective

I began my doctoral work firmly rooted, yet unsatisfied, with the Reformed tradition. While I remain a Presbyterian teaching elder, I find myself in a state of personal theological reformation. This began for me with the introduction of process theology[1] in my doctoral work. Through this system of belief, I found myself claiming a new theological home. As I explored the various ideas presented by process theologians, I found ideas about God, the world, and humanity that I could claim as my own with intellectual honesty. More importantly, I found a God whom I believe is worthy of worship. For me, process theology offers a vision of the world and the divine–human relationship that satisfies many of my curiosities; at the same time, it sparks a passion in me to live better and more responsibly in response and gratitude to God. Before we jump into the ideas about God and world that excite me, I want to briefly look at the philosophy I find so compelling.

Like many of our theologies, process theology is the result of a conversation between a people of faith and a system of thought. Process thought began as a "comprehensive vision of reality"[2] proposed by Alfred North Whitehead (no relation). He described his work as an effort "to generalize our knowledge, to seek a way of understanding the world as comprehensively as we can."[3] In the most basic sense, Whitehead's conclusions about the world describe it as an infinite series of interrelated experiences. According to Whitehead, "The elucidation of immediate experience is the sole justification for any thought; and the starting point for thought is the analytic observation of components of experience."[4] Human beings reflect and seek to make sense of all the moments of our lives, and we begin each reflection with the moment in front of us. Every moment (no matter how large or small) contains possibility as we take apart and put together each experience. There are possibilities that we act upon; there are possibilities we eschew; there are known possibilities and unknown possibilities; all of these are based on the past moments, reflections, and decisions that bring us into the present. Our life consists of our dynamic relationships with every moment. Any ideas we have are related to these moments in life; any illuminations we can conceive, believe, or receive center on these experiences. Our lives bustle with our connections to the world, to each other, and to the divine. Philosophies and even theologies often begin with these droplets of experience that ripple throughout our lives.

According to process philosophy, we organize the world around our reflections and meaning-making related to our experiences. We break down our experiences into ever-smaller parts, seeking to understand the dynamics at play in each moment of our lives. The world we live in is made up of a plethora of these small occasions of experience to which meaning is given. Out of these moments where the past and present collide, beliefs rise and fall; our memories are recalled, forgotten, and reshaped, and our imagination creates novel possibilities that propel us into the future. The dynamic movement of life, the becoming of persons in relationship to the world, is paramount to process thought and theology. This is in contrast to theologies and philosophies that, in Robert Mesle's words,

> give primacy to Being over Becoming, to independence over relatedness, to things over processes, to the idea that the human spirit is fundamentally isolated from the social and natural web in which we clearly live and move and are becoming.[5]

Simply put, life is a series of interrelated processes; it is comprised of movement; and, all that we experience is done in community with one another. Moreover, it is not just life that is interrelated. Rather all things are interconnected, from science and theology to people and the earth. We live together as an interconnected whole; our world is comprised of interdependent, interactive, and intertwined relationships. Not only does process theology provide us a way of thinking about the world dynamically, it is especially helpful because of its interdisciplinary approach to knowledge.[6] It is not a theology built apart from other disciplines, but draws from science, theology, psychology, philosophy, and sociology to help undergird the way it talks about the divine-human relationship.

However, using process theology often means standing in contrast to traditional (sometimes called orthodox) ideas about the divine and its relationship to humanity. These traditional theologies often describe God as unchangeable and controlling; some perpetuate the ideas from our early Greek heritage that God is omnipotent (all-powerful) and independent; while others continue to understand God as only male.[7] Process theology seeks to see and understand God and God's activity differently.

A PROCESS GOD

Omnipotence (all-powerfulness) and Omniscience (all-knowingness) are two attributes often used to describe God in traditional theologies. They are also terms and ideas that many process theologians seek to redefine, reimagine, or just plain do without. In this case, we are going to work on reimagining these terms in ways that help us better understand a third "omni"—God's omnipresence. Responses to process theology have ranged from acceptance to rejection to confusion. Many of the ways it seeks to redefine the above terms challenge long-held beliefs. Yet, process theology plays a significant role in helping us transform and redeem the emotion of fear. Its attention to the complexity of the world provides fertile ground through which we can explore and imagine the myriad ways that God connects to this world and interacts with humanity. Put simply, through the lens of process theology, we can imagine a place where fear and hope reside together.

A brief description of our journey through some of the ideas in process theology is in order. First, I will begin with a discussion of the problems with our current concepts of power, a discussion that leads me into examining the ideas surrounding a dipolar (immanent and transcendent) God. Moreover, it calls into question ideas about God's relationship to the past, present, and future. As we explore these ideas about omniscience, it becomes apparent that for hope, human possibility, and responsibility to exist, we must understand God's relationship to the future differently. This discussion comes full circle as we reimagine God's power as relational rather than coercive. As this conversation progresses, a process understanding of human activity, responsibility, and interaction with the divine develops. Out of these conclusions, we can start to understand human freedom, creativity, and power, which in turn ground our understanding of fear and hope. At the conclusion of this chapter, I will provide a synopsis that draws all of these constituent parts together into a cohesive vision for us to carry forward into the remaining chapters.

OMNIPOTENCE

Writing about the concept of God's omnipotence, theologian Daniel Bowman (2006) says:

> If God is all-powerful, then it follows that human beings are none-powerful. Even if we might be allowed some limited causal efficacy in our immediate environment, we are certainly bereft of true power: the power to determine one's own fate or to effect real good or progress in the world. (p. 14)

In traditional theologies, one of God's enduring characteristics is this idea of omnipotence. God's power is the power to control, to create, to manipulate, to destroy as God sees fit. As Bowman points out, to say this about God means believing that we are powerless. It can mean that we do not have to take responsibility for our actions, since God will work it all out; it can mean that nothing we do changes anything, so why bother trying; or it could mean that we have no real opportunity to make meaningful decisions about our lives. To say that God is all-powerful is to effectively remove any role or responsibility we might have in shaping this world. Why bother evangelizing, recycling, preaching, teaching, sharing, or loving if God already has things under control? For God to be all-powerful, as is often claimed, we must be willing to recognize our powerlessness. Is our every step and word a foregone conclusion? Would every experience happen regardless of our attempts to stop it? Process theologians often refer to this kind of power as the power to coerce; that God, having foreordained the movements of the world, makes us act in certain ways. This idea about God's perfect power relies on a very traditional, human, and hierarchical understanding of power.

Talking about these traditional forms of power, Robert Mesle points out that "people work toward the idea that power is the ability to affect others without being affected by them."[8] This is the power to coerce and the power to control; it is a type of power that trickles downward; it is a unidirectional power utilized unilaterally. This unilateral and unidirectional power assumes a single controlling element or force. All that has, is, and will occur is under the direct control of that force which holds the power. Thus we find ourselves in a constant search for power and the ability to control and shape our surroundings. Humanity, in living out this form of coercive power, often forgoes the call for compassion and relationship in order to increase their level of control.

This traditional idea about power has been co-opted into our understanding of God's omnipotence. Perfect power, according to many traditional theologies, becomes the power to control perfectly. When we begin to talk about God as omnipotent, as unilaterally powerful, then God becomes a benevolent tyrant and dictator. According to theologian Wendy Farley, "Omnipotent sovereignty is not the power of a love that values creatures; it is the benevolence of a slave owner, who is 'kind' to slaves but still deprives them of dignity and responsibility."[9] While we like to discuss the compassionate things that happen in this world as having their source in God, under this definition of power we cannot escape the fact that the cruel things are God's doing as well. It would seem that to believe in omnipotence as it is traditionally conceived would call into question the quality of God's love.[10] As Mesle argues,

> To be fully unilaterally powerful, I must not be affected by people, and that means I must not care about them. Healthy caring love is just the opposite: the more we love, the more we open ourselves up to being affected by the other.[11]

Faced with the realities of suffering and unpredictable tragedy, it becomes difficult to hold together concepts of a loving God whose power is coercive. Moreover, I find it hard to believe that such a God would be worthy of worship. Therefore, something has to give; either God is described as no longer completely loving, or the way in which we conceive of God's power needs to change. My choice is to maintain benevolence, compassion, and love as central qualities of God. This means that we must come to see power differently. We must break away from conventional and cultural definitions of power and reimagine it. The shift in thinking about God's power begins with understanding how God relates to the world and all of its many moving and working parts.

THE DIPOLAR NATURE OF GOD

The term *dipolar* refers to the two ways we understand God's nature—as *primordial*, abstract, and transcendent on one hand, and as *consequent*, concrete, and immanent on the other. For most process theologians, speaking of God's intimate and immanent presence in the world is second nature. One pair of theologians described God's immanence as "temporal, relative, dependent, and constantly changing. In each moment of God's life there are new, unforeseen happenings in the world which only then have become knowable."[12] It is as though God experiences the world in all its becoming, as it is becoming. With this idea, God's attributes move beyond an immutable passionless deity, putting God in direct relationship with the creation God loves so dearly. According to Robert Mesle,

> God is good because God shares the experience of every creature—every pain, joy, hope, despair, failure, and triumph. God is

not an *im*partial, *dis*interested observer of the world but the uniquely
"*omni*-partial" and *totally* interested participant in every relationship
there is. God knows what it is like to be you and me and "them" and
the animals and plants we all eat. In the fullest sense possible, then,
God is love: God is perfect relational power.[13]

Thus much of what we understand to be God's goodness hinges on God's
ability to relate to humanity and to the world. It is God's experience of the
depths of pain and passion in the world that emboldens God's compassion for
the world.[14] Furthermore, this compassion means little if it remains absent from
the world by the notion of an unmoved mover. The empath-ability of God is
directly tied to this immanent sense of God's being in the world with us.

This immanent quality is kept in check by the primordial (transcendent)
nature of God. At this pole, God is understood as timeless; God is "eternal,
absolute, independent, unchangeable. It includes those abstract attributes of
deity which characterize divine existence at every moment."[15] This is the sense
that God is bigger than just what is personal to me or to you. This includes
how we understand God as relating to the entire world as it has passed and as it
comes into being. Here, God is seen as omni-relational and more independent
of the world. When we talk about God's ability to know and be present to
what is happening everywhere in each moment, we are talking about God's
primordial nature.

Put these two ideas together and we paint a powerful picture of God.
This is a God who is able to intimately relate to the world in its entirety. A
God who can take in all of our experiences—whether pain, grief, joy, fear,
suffering, or pain—and exude the kind of empathic compassion needed in
response. This is a God who knows our experiences, as well as the history that
brought us to particular moments in time. God knows and is responsive to our
sufferings and joys; as we weep, God is moved to be present to our sorrow, fully
understanding its impact on our lives, and share the experience with us. The
same might be said for our struggles and our fears, that God is fully present to
the moments of our lives, receiving into God's self the impact of our experiences
and what it means to be us in each moment. Through the consequent and
primordial natures of God, we come to see God as ultimately relational in God's
own becoming, eternal yet changeable as the world continues to become. As
you begin to reimagine your understanding of what it means to be powerful,
consider these two ideas about the nature of God. How does having a God who
is intimately involved in the total experience of the world challenge traditional
ideas about power?

God and (in) Time

As we continue to reshape our understanding of power in relationship to God's activity in the world, one final component to examine is the relationship between God and time. Taking into account the dipolar nature of God, we can make some inferences about the past, present, and future. First and foremost, God operates in the present. We see this in the intimacy of the immanent nature of God. To be empathic is to hear what is happening at this moment in time and feel with someone through their experience. The ability to be present to the becoming of the entire world is also noted in the transcendent nature of God as well. In this we also see God's connection to the history of the world. God knows all that has happened, and all that is right now. Yet, can we say that God knows what is next?

In traditional theologies, the answer to that question is generally "yes." The way omniscience is often described includes the idea that God has knowledge of the future as well as the present and past. The difficulty with this is that if the future is known, then there is no logical way for there to be freedom for human beings. If God knows what is next, what we will do next, then the choices we make are mere illusions; the true work is done behind the scenes. This presents some difficulties to say the least. If the future is known, we are back to the idea that God's power is coercive. Even if the future charted before us is benevolent, it is nonetheless choice-less and powerless. We are marked for certain paths, pitfalls, and events. When the future is known, every journey is inevitable, and every experience inescapable.

This can be terribly comforting for many people, believing that everything is under God's controlling power. For some, freedom comes in believing that God knows everything about you from birth to death before you have even done it. At the same time, this kind of thinking destroys responsibility. If we cannot choose, we cannot be responsible for the actions we take, the words we use, or even the things we do that hurt others. There is no possibility for change, as people are set on a path and must follow it to the bitter end. God's knowing the future means that God knows the harm that will come to some people before it happens, and does nothing to stop it. Every bullet fired in war, every rape, every case of child abuse has been known from the get go. For me, I find this notion calls into question God's worthiness of worship. I simply find it hard to get behind the idea that a loving God knows the harm that will befall us and does nothing to stop it.

The allegiance to omniscience is puzzling. I can understand how comforting it can be to some, yet I cannot abide by it. As a process theologian, I see God's knowledge as perfect regarding the past and present. I also believe that the future is constantly opening before us. We are bound by the experiences and events that bring us to a present moment; experiences that limit the possibilities before us. At the same time, we do have choices. We do have some freedom and responsibility to decide the direction our lives will take. That is, given the experiences of our past, God works to offer us the best possible aim for a particular moment. Theologian Santiago Sia put it this way:

> God makes it possible for someone to do or not to do something. But the fact that one did something rather than something else or omitted to do it was that person's own choice. It was made by him or her and definitely *not* by God. God merely decided to make a number of alternatives open for that person.[16]

We rely on God for the best possible outcomes, but the choice to take a specific alternative is ours. Ultimately, we are responsible for things we do and say. Grace comes from the sense that we often fail in our choices, but God continues in relationship with us. God continues to attempt to persuade us into choosing the best of the alternatives available to us.

OMNIPOTENCE, REVISITED

The term that process theologians use to characterize the relational power of God is *persuasive*. When we emphasize an immanent God and an open future, we begin to see that the concept of coercive power is not a viable theological option. Yet, what does it mean to persuade? I think of persuasion as a respectful negotiation of power, possibility, and perspective. It assumes that both parties in a relationship have some power and interest in deciding a forthcoming action. To persuade is to provide possibilities while ultimately realizing that the party you are attempting to persuade has the capacity for self-determination; you may know what is best and seek to offer that knowledge, but they may choose otherwise based on their experiences. When we attempt to persuade someone, we assume that we have knowledge or experiences that will be helpful to that other person. Persuasion also assumes a shared relationship. It assumes that I care enough about you to attempt to help you see the possible alternatives outside the scope of your experiences. From the process perspective, persuasion forms the crux of relational power between God and humanity.

Robert Mesle describes relational power as

> (1) the ability to be actively open to and affected by the world around us; (2) the ability to create ourselves out of what we have taken in;

and (3) the ability to influence those around us by having first been affected by them.[17]

This idea of relational power is a radical departure from the ways we often talk about omnipotence. Here, to be in relationship is to be constantly negotiating power; we are to experience what another experiences, and be open to novel possibilities. Rather than assuming the height of power comes from the ability to command, this perspective sees the most effective form of power rising from our ability to be present and relate to one another and the world. For humans, relational power is limited by our experiences of the world.

How we understand God's power is vital to a life-giving faith. Theologian Daniel Bowman talked about God's power as extending "to the knowledge and perfect assessment of all possibilities for human beings, their communities, and their surroundings," and therefore "[human beings] cannot act in our own best interests, let alone in the best interests of those we love and those yet unknown, without connecting ourselves to divine power."[18] Here, relational power can be understood as the ability to relate and be related to perfectly; it is the power to experience and be experienced in our totality; it is an amazing opportunity to engage with God in novel and co-determinative moments that bring about greater beauty to a world that needs it. To see our relationship with God through the lens of relational power means understanding that God is truly with us, that God is truly for us, and that God cares and knows the pains of this world in meaningfully real ways.

If we can wrap our faith around God's interacting with the world in powerfully relational ways, then we open ourselves to seeing the possibilities in our midst. We begin to see how the world is shaped through responsible and irresponsible choices humans make; at the same time, we can have hope in the notion that God continues to offer novel opportunities in the experiences we face every day.

These novel solutions are often talked about as initial and subjective aims. The easiest way to define initial and subjective aims is by understanding their origination. An initial aim can be considered to be the best possible action offered by God at a particular moment in time. Some process theologians describe initial aims as "[t]he way that God is continuously active in the world by providing potentialities for becoming, which add value to the world and enjoyment to the experiencing subject . . . [it is] the infusion of value into the initial stage of an occasion's becoming."[19] Basically, in each moment, God's initial aim is to add value and meaning to our lives. These aims intend to bring about a greater relational beauty in both our experience and in the world's experience of us.

Initial aims are beautiful things; however, they are rarely fully realized. Instead, we most often enact what is termed a subjective aim. In each moment of our lives we face choices; we encounter competing aims that garner our attention. A subjective aim is the possibility we choose to act upon given the broad range of choices in front of us and the habits of life we have cultivated. As we know, not every subjective aim and its resulting choice and action is beneficial to ourselves and the world. As theologian Daniel Bowman puts it,

> Creatures with significant freedom, creativity, and power can destroy as rapidly and as thoroughly as they can create. Such creatures can also suffer in conscious, lasting, and perhaps inescapable ways; their pain detracts from the intensity of feeling God aims to achieve.[20]

The freedom to choose one subjective aim over another is a terrible liberation, fraught with celebrations and consequences. At times, the habits we have cultivated create more pain than enjoyment or value. We become caught in patterns that perpetuate destructive cycles of becoming. Moreover, the relational thrust of process theology means that the habits of community and culture can also limit our ability to respond effectively to our experiences. Bowman continues:

> Although forces beyond our control determine much about our situation and destination in life, even in the most constricted situation there is always something over which the human being, and the human being alone, has power.[21]

If we are locked into a past filled with abuse, it narrows our vision of the possibilities in front of us; until we can understand our own value, dignity, and worth, many of our subjective aims will develop through lenses of powerlessness and hopelessness. Even when we can realize some possibilities, cultural histories can impede progress toward realizing the possibilities of initial aims in our lives.

Hidden in the rhetoric of initial and subjective aims are the real possibilities of human power and freedom. Human power under this guise is, according to Bowman, the power to respond to one's unique situation and to become that response. It is the power of self-determination. God's self-determination uniquely affects all creatures directly. My self-determination, in itself, has a far more limited effectual range. That does not make it any less worthy of being called with the same name and given its due respect.[22]

For process theologians, human power is the power of choice, including the possibility of novelty. It is a limited power, to be sure, but it is important nonetheless. It means that the script of our lives is still being written. It means there are choices; we can choose our responses; we can choose how we construct ourselves in new moments, in really meaningful ways that shape successive future moments; we can choose to act, speak, and interpret in ways that make this world a more beautiful and creative space for ourselves and the world that receives our choices. Realizing this power to self-determine can be a powerfully hopeful thing, especially for those who have experienced trauma or live under the thumb of fear. It simply means that the trauma doesn't fully define you, and the fear we experience can be transformed in meaningful ways.

PUTTING IT ALL TOGETHER: A GOD OF POSSIBILITY

Christianity, indeed most religions, have attempted throughout history to characterize the qualities of their deities. We scour the biblical and historical texts for glimpses of God's activity and character. The truths we share today are built upon the foundations of yesterday and projected into the future. Believing something is about risk: it is about taking a chance and describing the activity of God; it is about living in both the experiences and mysteries of faith. Theology is a search for understanding, walking along the edge of knowledge, faith, experience, and tradition while also eyeing the cavernous void of mystery that surrounds us. While we may never fully understand God's character, it does not hurt to try and discern as much as we can in order to live more faithfully.

In this and previous chapters, we have been developing a tentative picture of God's character. Realizing that what we know of God is incomplete (much like what we know of anything in the world), we endeavor nonetheless to describe and define. I have described God as empathically able, as compassionate, as relational, as persuasive, and as knowledgeable. There is nothing new about these descriptions of God. However, by claiming process theology as a source of knowledge, there are assumptions and ideas that reform the meaning of these words. So, let's put all of this together into a cohesive statement; from there, we can begin to speculate about how this can impact our understanding of fear and its relationship to hope.

First things first, God is compassionate and loving. I do not believe that this is out of the ordinary for most people to believe. God cares for us, truly and completely. This is seen in God's grace, forgiveness, and hope for a better world through the relationships we share with God and one another. God's love is expressed in immanent ways. God is active in, around, above, and throughout the world. This means that God knows the intimate details of our lives; how we got ourselves into certain situations; the habits we have developed to deal with our experiences. God experiences the love, the hate, the despair, fear, hope, and joy that we live with daily. The mutual experience of empathy ties us to God in relational ways that go far beyond a mental and confessional life together. God doesn't just know our sins, God feels our pain; indeed God feels the pain, suffering, joy, and hope of the entire world. As Robert Thompson states:

> If God suffers, and particularly if God suffers on account of the world, then we humans are reassured of God's care, which provokes feelings of assurance. Furthermore, as creatures made in God's image . . . humans can also be reassured that, as God suffers, suffering will sometimes be our experience, and we can manage it with God's ever-present offerings of help. . . . Whitehead writes, "God is the great companion—the fellow-sufferer who understands" (Whitehead, 1978, p. 351).[23]

Thinking of God in this way means letting go of the idea of a distant creator or cosmic clockmaker; it means risking that God knows and feels the experience of the entire world, and that God's care and concern is more than just lip service.[24]

Saying that God is empathic and compassionate should have an impact on how we understand God's power. That is, when we understand and can incorporate another's experience into our lives, there is an opportunity for a relationship. We become less likely to coerce and more likely to cajole. Empathy and compassion require us to relate; they are necessary components of mutual and co-determinative relationships, and they affect how we use power in those relationships. Likewise, God exercises a relational power with the world, seeking to persuade us into new and more creative ways of responding to our experiences.

In addition, relationships require flexibility and adaptability. As we incorporate portions of others' experience into our own understanding of the world, we must be free to adapt and create. God's power to persuade us into enacting particular initial aims is met by our own power to choose. As we subjectively act in particular ways, God continues to be a steady compassionate presence that offers new aims based on the choices we make. Furthermore, God's power to relate is a power to relate to the entire world. We might even consider God omnipotent, inasmuch as God is able to exercise a relational power with the entire world. Thus the experiences of a heaving and breathing, creative and destructive world are "incorporated" into God's self, enabling God to relate even more intimately with our experiences and offer the best possibilities for our future.

It is in God's relationship with the future that we ultimately find freedom for humanity. If we shift our thinking to understand God's power as relational, then we need to understand what it means to be free. Freedom is not an anything-goes proposition. Just as I do not have the freedom to choose to be a bird, I do not have the freedom to escape an interrelated world—a world that constrains us, a world where we are coerced by powerful influences in culture, politics, and communities. We are constantly influenced, and even constricted, by these systems of power, and they influence our habits of thought and action. In contrast, there is freedom to be found in faith; this is the freedom to create with God's help. It is the freedom of novelty. Because the future is unfixed, we have some freedom to respond in unique and creative ways that can redefine us in relationship to certain situations. God becomes a God of possibility as we seek to live in faith. Robert Thompson describes God as being able to offer

> the best possibilities for that entity's future based on that entity's accumulated past; God's offer—God's aim—will reflect that entity's "given" situation but God's aim will also transcend that "given," because God seeks the best for all in all moments.[25]

Our human freedom and even hope to a certain extent is constrained by powerful conflicting systems. Yet, God's ability to create and provide novelty is unconstrained; it is the power to offer the best possible solution given the circumstances that brought us into a particular situation. Understanding God in this way means painting a different picture of how God is active, powerful, and present in the world.

Through this vision we can begin to create a new way of thinking about fear, one that incorporates it into our lives adaptively, rather than maligns it. An empathic, compassionate, relational God knows what it means to be afraid. This same God knows its usefulness and its abuse in the world. This same God may even offer fear as the most adaptive initial aim, given certain situations we face in a sometimes hostile and unpredictable world.

That is a loaded statement, I know. To say that God knows what it means to be afraid is not a stretch. If we endeavor to believe in any sense of an *Imago Dei*, we cannot pick and choose the parts of humanity that are fitting for an image of God. To believe in the image of God, however faulty that image may be, is to make some assumptions that the qualities that make us human are understood by a God who functions creatively in the universe. Thus to say that God understands what it means to be afraid is not really a stretch. Process theology stretches our imagination by putting forth the idea that God experiences the fear we feel and empathizes with us in those moments. This is how I understand the concept of Emmanuel, or how I understand that God is with us.

God is not some disinterested party in my life. I choose to believe that God knows what it is like to be me, and that God experiences the joys, struggles, trials, tribulations, and celebrations in real ways just as I do. In addition, God feels what it is like to experience these things. All we need to do is peruse scripture to see God acting and responding to the experiences of the world in emotional ways. In my estimation, God knows what it means to be afraid. God knows its usefulness; when it has been abused; and when it is time to move through the fear rather than ignore it. This experience of God should not be too much of a stretch for us.

What may stretch our imagination uncomfortably is the idea that God may use fear as an initial aim in our lives. My sense is that God relates to the world and humans by "offering the best possibilities for that entity's future based on that entity's accumulated past."[26] Who we are in a given moment is in part based on our experiences to that point in life. We change, we grow, we shrink, we isolate, we relate, we overcome, and we do all these things carrying the weight of our experiences wherever we go. In the midst of all of this, the God who is with us, the God who experiences life as we do, stands ready with possibilities meant to bring about a greater harmony for our lives and for the world. These initial aims may also include moments where fear can be the most adaptive and harmonious response to an experience in our lives.

The hypothesis is simply that God can utilize the emotion of fear and its behaviors to protect us. This is done in order to bring about the best possible future for a given circumstance. Seen this way, the emotion of fear is an adaptive and useful emotional state, beneficial to our ability to survive and cope with the world. These benefits would be unavailable if we ignored or suppressed the emotion. At times, the emotion of fear is a helpful initial aim that can increase the harmony and creativity of the world. Truthfully, there are times when the best way to relate to particular elements of the world is to avoid them. This is especially true for experiences where we encounter events that can be construed as evil or destructive to our lives and relationships. Being afraid can give us the insight we need to forgo a particular relationship in order to maintain the possibility of future interactions that benefit ourselves and the world. The interrelated world is far from perfect, and there are times when relationships collide and produce situations of threat and trauma.

If the emotion of fear can be seen as an initial aim in particular circumstances, then I believe we need to rethink our theological position on it. Fear, interpreted as a manifestation of God's love and relational power, may also be seen as a manifestation of God's hope and initial aims in particular situations. That is, our fears may be disruptive, but they may also reveal God's hope for our future and the relational possibilities of each new moment. When we are afraid we not only run from something, we are also running toward something. To be afraid biologically is to seek to preserve ourselves by surviving and coping with a threat. Yet, there is more to fear than just satisfying biologically driven needs. When we see fear through a theological lens, we add a layer of meaning to it. When we see fear as an initial aim, a layer of hopeful possibilities becomes apparent. Our actions in that moment of fear can direct us toward hope for the future. Even while we fight, flee, freeze, or appease, there are latent hopes that direct our energies through this experience. If it were not so, then the need for survival would be minimal. We need to be afraid; we need to understand that God might use fear to direct us to the best possible outcome in certain situations; we need fear, at times, to remind us what is worth living for in this world.

QUESTIONS FOR REFLECTION

1. Think about how you might describe God to others. What qualities immediately come to mind?
2. As you read this chapter, what were the similarities and differences in our visions of God?
3. What are the most important ideas about God for you? How do they impact your faith and your response to your experiences in life? How do they shape your words and relationships?
4. In what kinds of experiences can you imagine God using the emotion of fear to protect us and offer us hope?

Notes

1. Process theology is a term that is derived from the generalized terms of process thought and philosophy. In a succession of writings that began with Alfred North Whitehead's works, various theologians began to adopt and appropriate this system of thought for a more decidedly Christian audience. Whitehead's student Charles Hartshorne began this process of refinement that continued with John Cobb and David Ray Griffin, who wrote an introductory text in the mid-1970s. Today there are numerous strains of thought within process theology as people have continued to shape and reshape how it impacts Christian thought and practices.

2. Robert Mesle, *Process-Relational Philosophy: An Introduction to Alfred North Whitehead* (West Conshohocken, PA: Templeton Foundation, 2008), 4.

3. Ibid., 12.

4. Alfred North Whitehead, *Process and Reality*, corrected edition, ed. D. R. Griffin and D. W. Sherburne (New York: Free Press, 1985), 4.

5. Mesle, 9.

6. I find that process theology is one of the few theologies that take science seriously. A lot of work has been done regarding the connection between these two cognate disciplines. Books by Ian Barbour and David Ray Griffin are especially helpful in connecting these two disciplines. While there is not the time or space to elucidate the complicated arguments that undergird the connection between process thought and scientific pursuits, much of their work has helped me draw connections between neuropsychology and theology.

7. John Cobb Jr. and David Ray Griffin, *Process Theology: An Introductory Exposition* (Philadelphia: Westminster, 1976), 8–10.

8. Mesle, 65.

9. Wendy Farley, *Tragic Vision and Divine Compassion: A Contemporary Theodicy* (Louisville: Westminster John Knox, 1990), 93.

10. Even the argument that God may somehow limit God's power in the interest of freedom ultimately fails if we cannot give up traditional notions of God's omnipotence. Some may simply pose the question of "why bother," or see God's power as a mystery we aren't intended to understand. Our experiences, and the cognitive and emotional capacities to interpret and creatively react to them, are relatively unique within the universe we understand. We should acknowledge, at some point, that the mystery is beyond our knowing. We should also reach and stretch our capacity for knowing to its human limits before acquiescing and giving up knowing the qualities of God we can surmise from the world and its interrelatedness. That said, as we continue to better understand the world and the God who moves within and outside it, this God should exhibit some logical coherence without overestimating the impact of mystery as a fallback position.

11. Mesle, 70–71.

12. Cobb Jr. and Griffin, 47.

13. Mesle, 86–87 (italics author's).

14. We might think of Jesus as an example for this. We often talk about Jesus as fully human and fully divine; it is not such a stretch of the imagination to think of God as being able to experience the happenings of the world. Unless we are willing to assume that Jesus forgets everything at the resurrection, then all of his experiences, including his emotional life, have been incorporated into the experience of God in this world. In process theology, the immanence of God is a continuation of this kind of experiencing of the world. Indeed, I understand process theology as seeing God present through all moments of time up to the present.

15. Cobb Jr. and Griffin, *Process Theology*, 47.

16. Santiago Sia, *God in Process Thought: A Study in Charles Hartshorne's Concept of God* (Dordrecht: Martinus Nijhoff, 1985), 79.

17. Mesle, 73.

18. Daniel Bowman, "God for Us: A Process View of the Divine-Human Relationship," in *Handbook of Process Theology*, ed. Jay McDaniel and Daniel Bowman (St. Louis: Chalice, 2006), 15.

19. Jay McDaniel and Daniel Bowman, "Introduction," in *Handbook of Process Theology*, ed. Jay McDaniel and Daniel Bowman (St. Louis: Chalice, 2006), 7.

20. Bowman, 18.

21. Ibid., 14.

22. Ibid., 14–15.

23. Robert Thompson, "Process Theology and Emotion: An Introductory Exploration," *Journal of Pastoral Theology* 15, no. 1 (2005): 25.

24. One of the most difficult aspects of process theology for people to grasp is what God does with the experiences that are incorporated into God's self. For most process theologians, God is changed by these experiences. This is evidenced in the novel ways that God continues to attempt to persuade us. As humans freely make choices, God's aims must change with each new decision; thus God's experiences of the world are affected, which in turn affects God's responses. With no set future, there is no need for a strict adherence to God's unmoving-ness.

25. Ibid., 22.

26. Ibid., 22.

6

Fear and Hope

If you have made it this far, I hope that you are coming to realize how complex our experiences of the emotion of fear can be. It is an emotion that we cannot just switch off, never to be experienced again. It is a part of the way our brains work, and it is part of the way we experience the world. When we are afraid, we are doing nothing more than acting upon an embodied emotion and embedded experience. Fear is as much a part of the *Imago Dei* as love, compassion, anger, and joy. We can no more escape the emotion of fear than we can stop breathing and hope to live.

When we experience fear, it shapes our beliefs about the world, and it focuses our attention on specific objects. Fear can strengthen beliefs; it can shape them; it can even cause us to push aside some of our earliest beliefs. Fear is a powerful motivator that helps us survive and cope with a sometimes hostile and unpredictable world. However, there is more to experiencing fear than just surviving and coping. If we reflect on our experiences of fear, I believe we come to understand how we can thrive and have hope in this same world.

WHAT IS HOPE?

I hope you continue reading; I hope you wrestle with the assertions I am making; I hope I win the lottery; I hope for world peace, that people love one another, or that the economically poor of this world are treated with the respect their humanity deserves. *Hope* is a versatile word that has come to be used to imply a lot of different things. I think when we use the word *hope* we are assuming a positive stance toward the future and what might be. Hope is often used in the context of dreams (winning the lottery, world peace) or more certain possibilities (that you continue reading and wrestling with this text). While there is nothing wrong with thinking of hope in this way, I think there is more to it than simply the unfulfilled wishes we carry with us. For hope to matter, I think it must add value to our lives, give us direction, and help provide meaning for the things we are passionate about. When we talk about human hope, there are two places to turn to understand it: psychology and theology.

Psychologist Erik Erikson called human hope "the earliest and the most indispensable virtue inherent in the state of being alive."[1] Hope is as much a part of our existence as any other emotional state of being. Erikson went on to define hope as "*the enduring beliefs in the attainability of fervent wishes, in spite of dark urges and rages which mark the beginning of existence.*"[2] Erikson, who is perhaps best known for his developmental theories, thought that hope was present in those earliest moments, days, and years of life. If this is the case, then every moment we live, there is the possibility of hope encroaching into our lives. To be alive is to hope; it is to believe in some of the possibilities our imagination constructs. Hope, according to Erikson, is how infants develop trust in the world around them. The early responses to an infant's hopes allow them to develop and continue to trust the changing world around them. I see Erikson's ideas about hope as being grounded in the possible and the probable.

When we look at Erikson's words above, we can see that hope has to do with the possibility of something occurring despite its absence in the present moment. When hope is about possibility, it refers to the desire for something specific to occur in the future. Our beliefs and wishes are two of the ways we hope for something's arrival or becoming in the future. Much like fear, hope has an object attached to it. A hope in the power of love or the meaning of a relationship can drive us to act in certain ways. A hope for a better life can push us to act, to study, to work toward a goal. Oftentimes, the possibility-making aspect of hope can ignite a passion within us toward completing a specific goal.

What makes hope unique from mere dreams or wishes is the probability with which it can be attained. Erikson talks about the idea of a hope being attainable. Hope is so much more than just wishing to win the lottery, or dreaming about world peace. As psychologist Ezra Stotland puts it, implicit in the meaning of hope "is an expectation greater than zero of achieving a goal."[3] The difference between hoping to provide for your family by winning the lottery or by working and saving is the probability of attainment. Moreover, the relative attainability of a particular hope can provide additional passion for purposeful behaviors. Much like fear, hope can order our responses to situations. Stotland continues by saying that "with hope, man [sic] acts, moves, achieves. Without hope, he [sic] is often dull, listless, moribund."[4]

When we can understand hope as living at the crux of possibility and probability, it takes on more emotional qualities. It becomes a state of being that directly affects the present with some idea about what is desired in the future. Truthfully, it has a lot in common with fear. In one article, a group of psychologists describe fear and hope as anticipatory emotions, meaning that they are emotions "currently experienced due to something that could happen in the future."[5] Thinking generally about hope and fear, we can begin to see some of the psychological ideas that tie them together. They both have objects that direct the attention, and they are both emotions that live in the present but also orient us toward the future. Much like fear, hope is more than just a psychological idea.

It is practically unimaginable to conceive of the Christian faith without hope. Yet we theologians often leave hope to the realm of possibility and the conceptual. In traditional theologies, hope is often seen through two lenses. The first is an eschatological hope that looks to a future fulfillment of God's promises; the second hope centers on a look to the past for a better vision of reality. Theologian Robert Brizee describes traditional theologies as seeing hope as "both looking forward and looking backward. This tradition is filled with the hope that there will be an end of time."[6] Traditionally, we have looked to the future only to see the possibility of the end; our hopes have compelled us to look to the past to divulge the probability of this occurrence, as well as seeking possible and probable ideas about the present.

Obviously, there are some issues with seeing hope this way. The wide-open future presented in process theology calls into question any perspective that describes the certainty of the end of time. Certainly it is possible, and it is often wished for by various religious entities; yet, its probability, especially in our lifetime, should always be in question. Why, for example, should we hope for something that can merely be wished for? It is not something that can be brought about by our efforts or actions. We can no more command God or force God's hand, than we can be coerced by God into certain actions.

If the certainty of our hopes for the end of time is called into question, then we might be tempted to turn to the past. We might hope to wander the hillsides with Jesus or witness the power of his words and the peace of his presence. We may romanticize the days gone by, and hope for their return. Yet, living in the past negates a sense of possibility or potentiality; it is almost entirely rooted in the probable. While we can learn from the past, a constant sense that things were better in those moments violates the "ongoing creativity of God. To place such emphasis on one particular historic time or one particular environment is to miss God's continuous creative activity in the world."[7] Therefore, it seems as though sticking with some traditional theological conceptions of hope may prevent us from really exploring its possibilities, probabilities, and potentialities.

Turning to process theology, we see that hope is bound by the idea that "there is a God who intimately relates with the world in each instant."[8] Human hope is directly related to the sense that God is truly *with* us in life. The concept of hope in process theology "lies in the creative process rather than what is created. Hope is in the dynamic, the bubbling, the self-creation of each moment."[9] These creative processes stem from an interaction with a God who knows our potential, and who intimately relates to us in order to bring about the most novel and creative possibilities. Hope, understood this way, means reaching for the possibilities of what may come given the probabilities of our lives in each moment. Perhaps just as importantly, it emboldens us to remember the presence of God when our lives break and our dreams die. In these moments, we can hold on to hope because God is present with us, continuing to provide and persuade us into choosing the possibilities found in God's initial aims.

Basing our understanding of hope on the creative activity of God means that we must take a more active stance toward life. Hope embodies "the elements of fulfillment and participation which gives this hope a processive character and makes it possible to interpret it in a process framework."[10] Much like psychological understandings of hope, a theological hope has both anticipatory and attainable qualities. Hope is part of a foundation of becoming. It is the sense that what is, is never fulfilled, and that there is more to come. Hope doesn't rest in the past and how things were better in another time, but looks forward as it brings the past with it in order to help us understand what is happening now and what may come next. For Christians, our attainable hopes should center on the constant possibilities laid before us by a persuasive God. Our hope rests on the next possibility that God may offer, anticipating that the novelty and creativity of God will bring greater harmony to the world through our lives.

To be hopeful in this world is to be passionate about the now and the next. Hope is an emotion that anticipates the next possibility, but also realizes the probability based on what brought us a particular moment. Hope flies into the stratosphere, but always keeps its feet grounded. Hope is meaningfully real only when the future is open. We have to believe that change is possible for hope to matter. When we are at our most hopeful, we are looking at the possibilities of each moment and acting in ways that co-create a more beautiful reality. When hope abounds, we look beyond ourselves and see the relational structures of the world, and we act in ways that strengthen this web of connectivity. This is how we know that fear, in the right context, is intimately tied to hope as well as to God's activity in the world.

FEAR AND HOPE

Given that our futures are open, our imaginations are rich, and our God relates with us and the rest of the world, I have come to believe that fear and hope are intimately intertwined. When I look at the behaviors we enact when we are afraid—fright, flight, freeze, and appease—I see a desire to live into the future. Certainly, we could say that all we are doing is giving in to the most basic activities shaped by an evolutionary past; that our ability to experience fear is nothing more than a deeply encoded desire to survive and propagate. The difficulty with that argument is that it assumes we are nothing more than animals; it assumes that we are guided by nothing more than biological structures and chemical reactions that produce specific responses in relationship to an object that threatens us. It says nothing about the fact that we are meaning-making beings. We not only react to the world, we seek to understand it and have it make sense. We not only live in the present and remember the past, but we project ourselves into the future. Neuroscience can tell us about the need to survive and cope with hostile experiences in the world. What it cannot tell us is why we bother surviving in the first place; or, why we continue to seek to thrive in a world that may have beaten us down and given us reason to fear the next moment. Those are questions of meaning.

We might look at the behaviors associated with fear and see that they pull us from the object that threatens our existence. However, I understand fear to be more than just a reaction to a threat; it is quite possibly the most hopeful reaction, born of God's initial aims, for a particular moment in our lives. Instead of only being about escape, as they are with most animals, these behaviors can direct us toward more life-giving opportunities. As I have stated before, we don't just run from something, we run toward something as well. These behaviors direct us away from something that may harm us, but they also point to our hope for living another day. In this way, hope and fear are really intertwined in our fearful experiences. Every time we experience the emotion of fear, there is an undercurrent of hope that resides with that experience. As we become afraid and behave in certain ways, our instincts for survival kick in. After we have survived an experience, we can then begin to look back and see the hopes that undergird our desire to act.

I am writing this on the heels of the shooting at the movie theater in Aurora, Colorado, where twelve people were killed and another fifty plus wounded. In the midst of the stories of grief and outrage, anger and disbelief, were reports about people who dove in front of loved ones to protect them from bullets. In the fear that encompassed the room, their decision was to protect someone they cared about. This can be interpreted in a variety of ways, and if you were to talk to ten different people you might get ten different answers to the question why they might behave in this way. As I look at events like this, I see the closeness of hope and fear in such moments. Remember, hope is about possibility and probability. Therefore, in this line of thinking, the fear that fights the violence of that moment also imparts a hope of the possibility of survival for another.

Some might simply point to that as courage—but courage requires hope, and the simple belief that survival has a purpose. As I continue to look at fear and its meaning for our lives, I keep coming back to the idea that it is the undercurrent of hope in our fearful experiences that provides the impetus for our actions in the face of a threat. To see fear in this way is to believe that through our biological propensities, a thread of possibility is woven. It is to believe in what we are as humans, but also endeavor to see how our life is impacted by the meanings we create to interpret the world.

This intertwining or undergirding of hope and fear is vital to our ability to make sense of what it means to be afraid. The redemption of fear as a meaningful emotional state for Christian life and faith rests on our ability to understand it as useful, adaptive, God-given, and ultimately a fulfillment of God's aims in certain situations. When we begin to use language to describe fear in this way, we can begin to see its hopeful origins and the possibilities it can engender.

As we look back over the neuropsychological research on the emotion of fear, we can see how its conservation in human evolution has given us a tool for an almost automatic response to threats in the environment. The emotion of fear is useful in that it helps us survive when these threats loom before us. The unique fears that we recognize as individuals help us see its adaptive qualities. We do not fear the same things, nor do we react with the same intensity to specific objects in our environments. For better and worse, the emotion of fear adapts to the stories we tell about specific objects, ideas, or experiences. It helps us cope with a changing world and a variety of threats that could impact our lives.

Any form of belief in the *Imago Dei* is incomplete without proper attention and incorporation of the varying emotions we all have. We cannot like certain emotions and discount others if they make us feel uncomfortable. We cannot say that joy is a God-given emotion without also confirming the same about anger; likewise, we cannot give hope a privileged spot in an emotional hierarchy without giving fear a similar spot as well. All of our emotions are a part of the relationship between God and humanity.

Finally, to redeem fear and understand the undercurrent of hope that is present in these moments as well, we must begin to see God as a God of possibilities—an ever-present help if you will. I have talked about God as intimately aware and involved in our lives. A God who knows our past and present and is constantly offering the best possible future choices based on these circumstances. A God who is active and relationally powerful would use the fullness of our human capacities to offer the best choices available. This may even include utilizing our capacity for fear in order to protect and save us for other relational possibilities. That is, responding in fear may be the most hopeful thing we can do at certain points in our lives. The undercurrent of hope in these fearful moments helps us see that we might thrive by redirecting our energies in the world through a fearful response to a threat. While the undercurrent of hope is vital to giving fear a new meaning structure, hope also serves as an antidote to the persistent level of fear that seems to garner so much attention nowadays.

As an antidote, hope provides an alternative vision of reality that takes our fears seriously as one avenue of meaningful interpretation, but not as the only avenue of meaningful discourse. In times of great fear, we may turn to hope to help us find a greater purpose. Fear and hope are both emotions that anticipate. They are grounded in present possibilities and probabilities but often look to the future for the impetus to act. In this way, fear may ground some of our hopes, and hope may lift us beyond the veil of fear we are experiencing. Hope and fear, as described here, are emotions of activity. Hope is not synonymous with dreams, but requires a movement toward the possible and even probable in our lives. Thus fear and hope have significant action associated with their rise and fall. Both emotions give us the energy and passion to drive toward a perceived goal. Often these goals might even be similar as they revolve around survival, coping, and thriving.

This relationship between fear and hope is predicated on the idea that fear is utilized as it is intended. Unfortunately, that is not always the case. In the next chapter, we will explore some of the ways that fear has been abused, with the hope of developing a public theology of fear. If we are to truly grasp the possibilities inherent in an adaptive and useful fear, we must begin to see how it is abused in our public discourse as a nation and as faithful communities. Though fear is meant to guide and direct our attention, as we saw in an early chapter, it has become such a ubiquitous part of our cultural discourse that it is often left to run amuck. We must find a way to turn off or transform our fear-based narratives if we are to truly harness its potential and its hopeful capacities.

QUESTIONS FOR REFLECTION

1. How do you understand hope, especially in the context of your faith?

2. How are your hopes evident in the ways you act in the world?

3. Think about a time when you were frightened. How did you react? Which of the four defensive behaviors comes closest to your actions in those moments?

4. Reflecting on that same situation, are there hopes that you can point to in those moments as well?

5. What thoughts or relationships enabled you to pull through that experience?

6. When you think about this idea that our hopes and fears are intertwined, how might this help you interpret some of the threats and traumas we all face on a daily basis through the media we consume?

Notes

1. Erik Erikson, *Insight and Responsibility: Lectures on the Ethical Implications of Psychoanalytic Thought* (New York: W. W. Norton. 1964), 115.

2. Ibid., 118 (italics author's).

3. Ezra Stotland, *The Psychology of Hope: An Integration of Experimental, Clinical, and Social Approaches* (San Francisco: Jossey-Bass, 1969), 2.

4. Ibid., 1.

5. Hans Baumgartner, Rik Pieters, and Richard Bagozzi, "Future-Oriented Emotions: Conceptualization and Behavioral Effects," *European Journal of Social Psychology* 38 (2008): 685.

6. Robert Brizee, "So Then, Where Is Hope Today?," in *Reflections on the Relational Vision*, ed. Process and Faith (Claremont, CA: Process and Faith, no date), 2.

7. Ibid., 2

8. Ibid., 1.

9. Ibid., 3.

10. William Beardslee, *A House for Hope: A Study in Process and Biblical Thought* (Philadelphia: Westminster, 1972), 131.

PART 4

Responding to Our Fears

The goal of this final section is to begin thinking about transformative responses to the fearful stories we live day in and day out. The passion for life that runs concurrently in moments of fear can provide novel insights that may help shape our interpretations of the world. In these final three chapters, I develop a robust way of thinking about the fears and hopes that inhabit our lives.

In chapter 7 we explore ways to make stories of fear more complex. The plan is not just to juxtapose stories of hope alongside those derived from fear; it is to see that those stories were present all along and how to access them. Fear often creates a myopic view of the world that crowds our memories of certain events. This chapter explores some methods of complicating stories of fear, which can, in time, mitigate their impact.

Chapter 8 looks more closely at two proactive responses to fear-based narratives: resistance and resilience. Resistance can be thought of as the ways we actively and implicitly transform our fears. Resilience is the stance toward life that we assume in response to the narratives that haunt us.

The final chapter explores the ways powerful influences manipulate the emotion of fear in order to render communities helpless and powerless. Here, the discussion shifts to how individuals and communities can respond to these attempts to abuse our capacity for fear. Looking back to the biblical witness, we will explore how we might understand fear from a relational standpoint. Furthermore, we will explore how perfect love may drive out fear, as well as one vision of what perfect love may look like.

7

Telling Ourselves a More Complex Story

Words matter, a lot. Words form the backbone of the stories we tell, and stories are essential to our ability to relate effectively to the rest of the world. The words we use to tell a story shape what it means to us and to those who hear it; and, how we respond to stories can tell someone whether we are a safe person to talk to or not. Stories help us organize the meaning of our experiences as we construct and reconstruct reality in every moment. The stories we tell can create or destroy, mend or bruise, inspire or incite. As Australian philosopher Kim Atkins says, "to the extent that a life is coherent, it is so because it deploys narrative strategies, and for this reason, narrative coherence is crucial to agency, moral identity, and, ultimately, a good life."[1] Our lives and our identities are built one story at a time, both those stories we tell and those we hide. Like a good book we constantly add chapters to our lives, building one story upon another, creating habits, worldviews, and hopes. Each moment contains the seeds of a new story and the presence of a dynamic actor living out these stories.

Yet, there is a caveat to this narrative lifestyle; each and every story we tell is incomplete. No story tells the entire truth of an event. No one captures every detail, especially when fear or other powerful emotions grip them. Talk to ten people about an experience and you will get ten different interpretations, ten different descriptions, ten different degrees of emotion, and ten different meanings and lessons. Stories are as unique as the people who tell them. This is why our fears are unique, and trauma is so subjective. We all have different stories, habits, ideas, resources, and roadblocks that shape our interpretations of an experience; we are people who live in specific contexts, who also come from specific contexts.

Our stories are not just the products of a single person; they are created in the context of lived relationships. Pastoral theologian Andrew Lester puts it this way: "Though each person brings individuality to the creation of personal stories, these stories are not created in isolation. The mind never works completely free of existing perspectives, but is constantly influenced by our social context and personal history."[2] Simply put, while the stories we may tell are uniquely ours, they are created in relationship to our past, our perspective, and the people around us. What we can take this to mean is that every story is more complex than the details, relationships, situations, and emotions we remember or share with someone else. We tell the truth from what we know; yet, what an experience encompasses is far more vast than the truths we are able to share. Furthermore, in the midst of trying to capture the details of an event, our emotions shape what we might remember.

In particular, fear enables us to home in on certain specifics of an experience. This embodied emotion, when it works as it should, narrows our vision of an object, idea, or person that we feel threatens us. We focus on specific details, often in spite of the many things happening in the larger environment. Our fearful stories are often shaped by the intensity of the emotion, the specific details we can make out, as well as any memory we connect with in that moment. Survival often takes on a prominent role. We might look for ways out, physically and/or mentally; we may decide to fight or appease a threat, as they offer the best opportunity for continued existence; small details in our surroundings loom larger as we seek something that may help us cope with the overwhelming flood of stimuli from our newly awakened bodies.

The narrow view of the world offered by a fear-based narrative often excludes real and meaningful experiences that balance it out. The power of these emotional stories to consume or create beliefs about the self and the world can feel overwhelming. Yet, even with a story developed out of fear, there is always more to remember. There are details about the experience and our actions within those moments that we gloss over or even deny. With every story, there are numerous counternarratives—alternative stories running with and against a prevailing memory—that offer alternative perspectives of an event. These subplots or minor narratives give us an opportunity to open ourselves to transforming the passions of fear into the hopes that have been present all along. Ultimately, it is our ability to add layers of complexity to these fearful stories or give life to the counternarratives that enables us to enrich our experiences and reclaim the goodness of life.

SANDRA'S STORIES

Let's talk about Sandra again. Remember, she was the one who stumbled into your office, exhausted and forlorn. She slumped wearily into the chair across from your desk; and, with great effort, told you of being mugged outside her apartment while walking home from work. She proceeded to describe how she cannot be out after dark; how she is afraid of every shadow; how she no longer goes out with friends and has moved into the basement of her parents' house in order to feel safe again. Sandra explains that even in broad daylight she will jump when a man appears at her office door. She feels like she can't let her guard down, even for a second. She wants her life back; she wants to feel safe again; she wants to know that God is still there; in short, she wants to feel the hope, love, and faith that encompassed her life before this event occurred.

So, how do we help Sandra? What can we do as a pastor or friend to help Sandra make her stories more complex? In the aftermath of such events, our memories can focus in on details that make us feel powerless or helpless. Together these are powerful feelings that in turn can create an overwhelming sense of hopelessness. Helping someone see that there is more complexity to their story requires us to use our imaginations. I think the main things we can do are empathize, educate, and encourage. All three of these possibilities are meant to decrease any sense of shame Sandra might experience as a result of this fear-based story.

EMPATHY

Empathy goes a long way in helping us imagine what it must be like to experience such an event—how we might feel overwhelmed by feelings of guilt or shame. Empathy is the means by which we learn what it is like to be Sandra in that moment. It is devoid of the need to fix Sandra, or explain how she shouldn't be afraid or how much God loves her. When we find ourselves wanting to say things like this, it usually comes from our own need to feel safe and secure; furthermore, it is usually unhelpful, and the person receiving this kind of feedback may either brush it off or deem us unsafe to talk to.

We all can empathize with what it feels like to be afraid, mainly because we all have experienced moments of fear or terror. The main point of empathy is to relate; it is to remind someone of their humanity and the continued possibility found in caring relationships. It may mean pointing out to someone that feeling afraid at certain points in our lives is a perfectly normal and faithful response. Simply being with someone, walking the same path they walk, even if just for a little while, can help ease the burden of shame that is often heaped upon feelings of fear. If we can be present, mentally, emotionally, and even theologically, then we might bear witness to someone's efforts at transforming the fears that haunt them.

EDUCATION

Empathy is our first resource, but we also have a responsibility to educate; we have a responsibility to remind people of God's presence before, during, and after each moment of our lives. We cannot empathize with someone who has experienced trauma while at the same time deriding the emotion of fear. People need to know that it is okay to be afraid. We need to be able to tell people that everyone experiences fear, at least everyone with a brain. They should hear from pulpits, in classrooms, and in their relationships with one another that life is sometimes scary, and fear is a natural response to many of those moments.

We also need to share with people that we are more than a bundle of neurons; that the whole of our being is greater than the sum of our parts. Fear helps us adapt to our environments and survive an imminent threat; it also has the power to remind us of what is important. There are greater existential ideas at play when we seek to survive a threat. There has to be something to live for, something to be passionate about, something to guide our attention into a future imagined reality, or else we would succumb to the threat and cease to exist. Even a fear of death can be transformed into a hope for life. Fear is a passionate reaction to a threat that transforms our lives, identities, and the stories we tell; of course, I believe hope can be equally passionate and transformative.

This leads me to wonder about the neglect of emotions in most mainline churches. What is it that keeps us from embracing these embodied realities? Is it their power to shape reality? Is it their independent and often inconsistent nature? Have we become so dependent on our intellect and rationality, that we have forgotten that faith requires the risk of passion? We neglect anger and fear at the risk of alienating joy and hope. Yet, if we can educate, if we can direct people's attention to the possibilities inherent in these adaptive emotional states, then there is the possibility of transforming the passion they engender into constructive pursuits. This can only happen when we educate people as they traverse life.

If we have not chosen to educate ourselves and others about the transformative passion and power of emotions, our empathy and encouragement may ring hollow. The important words we choose to use in those moments may lack conviction and leave Sandra wanting more. Education begins with understanding what it means to be afraid, to be angry, to have sorrow, to experience joy. It means exploring these vital emotions through psychological and theological lenses. Learning about our embodied emotional life allows us to become more comfortable with these incredible sources of passion. Perhaps more importantly, knowing about these emotional states and finding constructive and transformative theological interpretations opens us to moving away from shame-based interpretations and into a productive relationship with our embodied selves.

ENCOURAGEMENT: RESISTANCE AND RESILIENCE

Perhaps one of the most important things we may be able to do is encourage Sandra. Empathizing with her situation and educating the shame away could prepare her to hear something novel. Stories of survival often include moments of resistance and resilience woven into their telling. However, we are often so focused on the emotion of fear (or resultant shame) that we forget or ignore those places where we actually have fought back against a threat or trauma. In the focused telling of our traumas and fears, we forget the subtle ways that we seek survival and adapt to cope. When we talk about the things that make us afraid, I think we often search out moments of power in our perceived powerlessness, hope in our understood hopelessness, or help in our helplessness.

Even when a story is shared and we feel utterly defeated, the simple fact that we were able to tell it can be a source of hope. That we had the courage to ask for help or the strength to endure life up to that moment, points to our resistance and resilience. If we were to go back over a story permeated by our fears, I think we would see the ways that we try to claim a sense of power. Despite being overwhelmed by the lens of fear, if we listen to our story we would hear cracks in the veneer. These small fissures of resistance and resilience speak of our attempts to breathe hope into the event. In the moment, when our fear is meant to be active and adaptive, we react in an effort to survive and cope.

When the moment has passed, it may be time to reflect on the possibilities of hope inherent in that moment. It is time to search out the layers of complexity that are already present. Once we allow ourselves to bear witness to a more complex reality, then we have some choices to make. Do we reject a hopeful counternarrative that makes a long-held and often secure position more complex? Do we hold tight to a persistent fear-based narrative in order stick with what is familiar? Can we accept ourselves as capable, empowered, co-creative actors in a sometimes hostile and unpredictable world? Can we risk believing in a present and intimate God who has never left our side? Taking up these and other minor subplots to the stories we have been sharing with one another complicates the often simplistic view of fear that we have. Finding alternative stories that run concurrently with those things we fear, frees us to transform the passion generated by fear. In this moment, we move from mere survival to grasping at the opportunity to thrive through the fear.

Moving from surviving to thriving requires us to juxtapose the adaptive qualities of fear that saved us in a particular moment with the relationships that made our life worth saving. As meaning-making creatures, we aren't just running from a threat, there has to be something worth running toward. In the crevices of our minds, there is a reason to fight for our survival. Fear and hope collide when we realize that, despite the selfish actions we sometimes take when afraid, there is more to the story than just me. There is something transformative about complexity, something constructive in realizing our resistant and resilient actions. This is not always easy though.

Sometimes it can feel as though stories of resistance and resilience are hard to come by and even harder to believe. This is where theology can help create some transformative fissures in our stories. One of the main sources of counternarratives of hope, strength, resistance, and resilience is found in the divine-human relationship. Juxtaposing a dominant fear-based story with one of God's enduring presence, love, and hope for our futures can add multiple layers of complexity. Together, these contrasted stories begin to flesh out the idea that a fear-based story is just one part of our lives. They reveal that the stories of our lives are born from the hopes God has for us, and that those narratives stretch beyond God's call to be afraid in one particular moment. Even as God might persuade us into utilizing the passions of fear to survive, there is an undercurrent of God's hope in these same stories. There is always the hope that we might thrive and engage the world in life-giving ways; there is always hope that we can end the relationship that threatens us and return to relationships that give us life and meaning; there is always hope to be found in remembering a God who knows perfectly the past and present, as well as what is required in order to move into the future in the best possible way. There may be no greater encouragement than to remind someone they are loved deeply and known intimately by a God who truly cares and knows what it means to live, feel, and move through this world.

TALKING TO SANDRA

How might we talk to a friend, a congregation member, even ourselves about a fear-based story? Using Sandra as an example, let's explore some options. I believe it begins with simply empathizing with her and trying to meet her in the place she mentally lives. I might remind her that fear is a natural reaction to the trauma she experienced—that even her feelings of powerlessness and helplessness are natural reactions to being violently violated. If she is struggling for a word or emotion, I might comment on how scary it must be to live with that kind of memory. Empathizing is not about fleshing out every detail or flushing out emotions, it is about entering the experience of someone else as an invited visitor and trying to find words to describe what you see. It may mean offering words to describe events while acknowledging that your interpretation is nothing but a guess, and that the person bearing the story has every right to correct and amend your observations.[3] Empathizing with another can empower someone to step beyond the shame they feel in sharing what they think is a weakness. It can also create the kind of space where education and encouragement may impact another's interpretations.

As a people of faith, our education often begins with talking about faith and God. We might remind Sandra that God was, is, and will be with her, regardless of how alone she might feel. If we feel she is ready to hear it, we might offer a theological interpretation that understands fear as a gift from God, that fear helps us respond to threats in our lives, and there is no shame in feeling afraid at various times in our lives. We might even offer that some people believe fear to be God's best hope in situations when our life feels threatened. That God's best help and hope in those moments is to enable our survival through being afraid. We might talk with Sandra about how our brains are wired to feel afraid; and, if fear is embodied in this manner, then who are we to say that God was wrong to give us this capability? We might even point out that often when we tell stories concerning fearful moments, we have a habit of focusing on particular details. In that same vein, we might wonder if there was any other story or stories that Sandra could recall that would help her keep trying to reclaim the goodness of life.[4]

Empathy creates a relationship; education prepares people for the reality of fear; encouragement reminds people of the possibilities of God's presence through the ways we resist and are resilient. In the end, it is encouragement through creating more complex stories that helps insert small rays of hope into fear-tinged stories. These rays of hope create a richer and more vibrant story and add layers of meaning that may have been brushed aside or forgotten. Of course, the caveat is our ability to be ready to change our stories and live in to newer ways of interpreting the world that reveal its more life-giving qualities. When we can begin to see our stories as more complex, then we are also able to see how we have been actively resisting and resilient in the face of these fears.

In order to encourage Sandra, I might acknowledge her courage to ask for help in bearing the weight of the story she shared with me. This is not a flippant compliment, but stems from my belief that she is fighting against cultural stereotypes that tell her she must bear and figure out things alone. There is also strength and resilience to be found in the fact that she continues to go to work and continues to try and find safe ways to live, despite the overwhelming sense of foreboding that dominates her interpretations of the world. Often, when we are looking for these moments of resistance and resilience, we are engaged in hearing the story as it is told, but also listening for the things that aren't being said.

Dealing with these stories is not only about personal empowerment, but also connecting people to life-giving relationships. In this instance, Sandra's parents, and their willingness to open their home to her, provide one avenue of exploration. We might explore what it means to her to have people who care enough to do what it takes to help their daughter feel safe again. We could encourage her to explore how her friends have reacted to this event in her life. In addition, we might speculate about what it means to those friends that she feels unable to go out at nights. What are they missing in not being able to relate to Sandra? As you can see, encouraging Sandra to take a broader view of the story can provide numerous sources of encouragement for her to explore life again. It also puts the story into the broader framework of her life, allowing it to have some power, but not total power.

Certainly there are acts that we commit under the pressure of fear that are less than helpful. Fear can lead us into isolation from meaningful relationships. It can drag us into a self-important centeredness where there is little regard for the common good. Yet, fear is also adaptive. It helps us survive and cope. Ultimately, it is redemptive in its ability to draw out of us our greatest hopes. Transforming the passion of fear into constructive relationships with the world and others can lead to novel ways of relating to one another. For individuals, there can be power in claiming fearful, traumatic, and threatening moments. There is no need to be ashamed of the fear we experience. At the same time, we must be cognizant of what that fear makes us do. Does it cause us to hurt others? Do we eschew the good of those around us in order to merely save ourselves? Fear and hope are both relational. They enter our minds through our relationship to the world. They form part of the backbone of our beliefs, thoughts, and imaginings. I have cautioned people before with the notion that it is perfectly fine to be afraid; however, living in fear is a whole different story.

QUESTIONS FOR REFLECTION

1. Think about a time when you were afraid. What do you recall experiencing in those moments? What did you feel in the moments after that experience?
2. Putting those two experiences together into one story, how does it create a more complex picture of what happened in those moments?
3. Of empathy, education, and encouragement, which seems the easiest or hardest to use in a caring conversation?

4. How would you express empathy and encouragement to Sandra? What words or statements would you use?

5. How have you laid the groundwork in your life or contexts for the experience of emotions as God-given and beneficial for our life together?

6. What do you find challenging or comforting about the idea that there is an undercurrent of hope in our fearful experiences?

Notes

1. Kim Atkins, *Narrative Identity and Moral Identity: A Practical Perspective* (New York: Routledge, 2008), 7.

2. Andrew Lester, *The Angry Christian: A Theology for Care and Counseling* (Louisville: Westminster John Knox, 2003), 93.

3. I often refer to this as being curious and stupid. We are to be genuinely curious about the experience of another. We take the position of wanting to know what it is like to be living with certain stories. Genuine curiosity doesn't seek to solve riddles or propose solutions. It should instead be coupled with a healthy dose of stupidity. As crass as it sounds, we need to take the position that we know nothing of what it means to be someone else. We are given the gift of bearing witness to how they work these stories into the larger framework of their lives. As we witness this work and offer observations and interpretations, we do so knowing and accepting that our offerings can be rejected, amended, or transformed. We need, as pastoral caregivers, to be okay with being wrong (even if we turn out to be right). We need to be okay with having someone sit across from us and tell us that what we said has no bearing on their interpretation of a story. Being stupid is holding on to the relationship with another without feeling the need to constantly defend our interpretations as the right way of thinking. To be able to correct perceived experts (whether we see ourselves as that or not) gives someone agency and empowers them to interpret their own stories anew.

4. This is not something I would recommend doing right away with someone who has experienced trauma. Only when they have had time to process the experience with a therapist or other mental health professional would I venture in this direction. As pastors or even as friends, we are often present for the spiritual crisis that someone is experiencing. They may be getting good therapeutic help (and if not, you can certainly encourage it). Given time to reflect, asking questions about how they experience hope in the midst of an overwhelming fear can begin to add layers of complexity to the stories they tell. Sometimes we just need to create the space for someone to tell their story.

8

Fear in the Public Sphere

What have we learned about the emotion of fear so far? Well, the emotion of fear is an embodied emotional state meant to help us survive, cope, and thrive in a sometimes hostile and unpredictable world. It can be an adaptive, helpful, and even creative response to many of the threats we experience. Furthermore, there is a link between fear and the hopes we live out in present moments and project into the future. At times, being afraid may be the result of God's best possibilities, and therefore God's greatest hope in particular circumstances. However, what about those times when it is not? What about the times when fear is abused by those with powerful voices in order to manipulate people into agreeing with certain remedies? What about preachers who use the fear of hell and damnation in order to garner more support for their causes and ideas? What about politicians who use the fear of terrorism to demonize religions or groups of people? What about pundits who manufacture fears in order to sell solutions and increase their own power?

As we move from this individual context to a communal one, I believe how we understand fear needs to be further nuanced in light of the current dominant North American culture. On an individual level, the adaptive and meaningful qualities of fear are far easier to see and its relationship to hope is easier to express. In communities, the emotion of fear can be adaptive, but it also can be abused. There are times when it is absolutely appropriate for communities to be afraid. Most often this is when communities find themselves in situations of violence or oppression. In these moments, fear is often about banding together to survive in the face of a threat. Fear, in these moments, can provide a powerful and passionate impulse to act in the face of danger. Moreover, as time stretches beyond the fearful event, communities can reflect and seek to reframe these fearful moments to express the hopes that run underneath their reactions. When whole communities are challenged by a threat that may signal their impending doom, then their communal experience of fear should not be denigrated. When violence threatens the fabric of a community and culture, fear can provide the kind of passionate response that enables a community to survive, cope, and, in time, come out thriving on the other side. It can serve as the catalyst for resistance and resilience in the quest for a just response to the violence. Fear can sometimes give rise to novel hopeful ideas and programs. When children are at risk for violence, safe after-school programs crop up; when violence and abuse occur in a community, we can often find dedicated groups of people who will risk speaking out to stem the tide of violence. One of the final steps in a narrative therapy experience is to challenge a person to utilize what they have learned in order to help others. This is mimicked in many communities, most recently in the messages of hope provided by those who experienced Hurricane Katrina to those who experienced Hurricane Sandy.

However, fear has also been used as a tool for manipulation in communities. Nowadays, it is not uncommon for groups to act out of a fearful place without real need or cause.[1] Think about the rhetoric of politicians around economic issues; these issues are often described as do or die, win or lose. The "fiscal cliff" of 2013, the yearly "war on Christmas," and issues around gay marriage are often described in terms that create the image of them as threats. These and other abusive stories of fear sow the seeds of discord, and create isolation and dread. In these situations, there may be good reason to begin reexamining the call to not be afraid; when we are obviously being manipulated to experience fear, we need to be reminded of the presence of a God who is with us wherever we go. However, there is more to responding to this emotional abuse; we must also be ready to respond to those who would manipulate us. We must be ready to stand up in the face of rhetoric that seeks to provoke the emotion of fear and dump it into the public sphere. To simply not be afraid is not enough to counteract these messages that seek to divide us through the manipulation of our fears.

On a public and communal scale, things become much more complex and confounded. What happens when people put forth fear-based narratives in order to offer their hope as the most viable solution? What happens when hopes compete with one another for supremacy? Thinking beyond my hopes and my desire to thrive throughout life require us to think about a public theology of fear and hope. Fear in the public arena can take on a different life. As social psychologists Konty, Duell, and Joireman have noted:

> Creating and sustaining this fear serves some of the most powerful interests in American society. The media are interested in cultivating fear because it sells more ads and publications. The more afraid people are, the more information they crave. Politicians are

interested in cultivating fear because it provides fertile ground to offer solutions. The more afraid people are, the more they crave solutions to the problem. . . . Commercial interests also benefit as people seek goods and services to make them safer. Finally, various governmental institutions benefit as they receive more funding to take care of the problem.[2]

In this day and age, our capacity for fear is manipulated and abused in order to manufacture particular cultural states of mind. By putting these narratives out in the public sphere, the hope is to keep us dependent on powerful people in order to feel safe. While there is nothing wrong with being afraid, there is something to be said about living in fear. We need a theological response to the intentional manipulation of our emotions, as well as a response to those who attempt to perpetuate that lifestyle. Furthermore, while we might rail against purveyors of fear, we must develop some sense of what it means to be hopeful in our communal life together.

THE FEAR OF CRIME

One of the preeminent fear-based narratives in American culture centers on the perceived pervasiveness of crime in our communities. We are taught through the lead stories of news outlets and plotlines of primetime shows that crime and criminals are everywhere. The sheer breadth of crime-related stories we are exposed to perpetuates a cultural narrative that is far more extensive than the actual incidence of crime in our lives. Over the years, social psychologists have studied the impact of these myths. From looking at a variety of studies about the effect of crime stories in the news, several themes emerge. The basic conclusion is that the more you know about crime, the more likely you are to fear it. These fears, in turn, lead us to restrict our social behavior, distrust our neighbors, and desire more punitive measures for criminal behavior.[3]

Our fear of crime creates an expectation that we will be victimized by crime. In turn, we develop myths about strangers and the lack of safety in the world; we prepare for what we feel is the inevitable and insulate ourselves, barring our windows and sleeping with guns under our pillows. In some cases we view our neighbors with suspicion, documenting their behaviors and comparing them to the narratives we hear about in the news or on the shows we watch. So rich are our imaginations about the impact of crime that the people who fear it most (women and the elderly) are far less victimized than the populations most impacted by crime (males and the young).[4] We have created whole crime-based communal narratives that stem from the fears raised by our exposure to a variety of media. These kinds of narratives are different from personal experiences with rape, murder, abuse, or burglary. Crime, as I talk about it here, refers to how the term is used generally to construct fears in the community, rather than specifically to talk about the impact on a victim's life. This can be thought of as similar to the distinction I made earlier between fear (as an embodied emotion) and fears (as uniquely subjective experiences).

The most interesting note in the social research is that the place where the fear-based narratives of crime are least effectual seems to be in those groups where people know their neighbors. The more a community is integrated, the more people know and trust their neighbors and are willing to intervene on their behalf, the less likely it is that a pervasive fear of crime influences their lives. To state the obvious, the relationships (or lack thereof) we share with the people around us often dictate how much power the rhetoric of a fear-based narrative has over our lives. Our ability to risk relating to the people around us seems to impact our ability live in more life-giving ways.

My spouse and I spent a good deal of time walking around neighborhoods before we settled on a place to live. It took two years for us to find the right house in a neighborhood of our liking. We walked and talked to people in many communities in Denver before settling on a general location. Eventually, we found a house for sale. It was smaller than we wanted, older than we had hoped for, and on a little busier street than we anticipated. However, it was the neighbors on the block that caught our attention. From our first walk down the sidewalk, people who lived there spoke to us. They told us about the area, about the street and its location, about its strengths and challenges. They welcomed us before we made the decision to stay. The day we moved in, there was an 8½- by 14-inch sheet of paper in our mailbox with pictures of every home on the block, along with names and phone numbers of the people who lived there.

Our block is an exceptional place to live, especially considering the myth of privacy and independence that permeates our culture. When a number of cars on our block were broken into, an email was shared between neighbors so that we could be on the lookout. When we are out of town, neighbors notice and look out for our house. Our kids play in the front and back yards, people say hello to one another, and we often gather on the sidewalk to check in with one another. Once a year, on Memorial Day, we have a party where the entire block is shut down and we just sit, talk, and share a meal. The kids play together in the street, while the adults listen to music and tell stories of the previous year.

It is in no way an idyllic community, but at the same time a little knowledge of one another has gone a long way in making it feel like a safe place to live and raise our children. On more than one occasion, when crimes have occurred in the greater part of the neighborhood, my spouse and I have remarked offhandedly that we feel lucky to live where we do with neighbors who watch out for one another. While my experience may be unique, it begs the question of what risks need to be taken in order to recreate communities that care for one another. Moreover, what is required of us as faithful people in order to creatively engage and transform the fear-based stories we encounter daily? To begin to answer these questions, we need to explore what it means to create public theologies.

PUBLIC THEOLOGY

Pastoral theology is a discipline that operates at both micro (individual) and macro (communal) levels. As theologians, we can't be content with merely appealing to individuals; the theological and biblical witnesses to which we often refer are documents written for communities, often by communities. Therefore, it is not enough to describe the impact of a phenomenon as being solely on individual minds and lives. Our work has to stretch beyond the framework of individual care and into the public space where larger systems impact our worlds and shape the stories we tell. We are all a part of the community, even as we are recognized for being unique in those relationships. Pastoral theologian Larry Graham notes that "to care for persons is to create new worlds; to care for the world is to build a new personhood."[5] As we explore this public domain, the focus of pastoral theology morphs into a theological discipline that "critically examines the organizing myths, symbols, and belief systems operating within caregiving enterprises, and seeks to modify these so that care might be more effective."[6] Thus pastoral theology in the public realm is about critically examining the myths that guide our cultural conversations, as well as offering methods for reorganizing these stories so that a greater level of care is present.

In essence, public theology attempts to tell a new story. It grafts itself onto the imagination of a culture and seeks novelty and creativity. When we accept these abusive stories of fear, we incorporate them into a theological life that shapes our actions and thoughts. They shade our imaginations, creating terrific and terrible outcomes. They can sometimes hinder our ability to see ourselves in others, and limit our capability of walking a mile in their shoes. Most of all, these stories impact our ability to relate meaningfully to our communities. When we adopt fear-based myths into our communal life, theological imagination, empathy, and interdependence seem to take a backseat in our interaction with the world.

A well-told story holds with it great power, whether it describes great fears, hopes, loves, anger, or joy. When we incorporate a story into our lives it is interpreted through lenses of meaning that shape its value and purpose for us. As pastoral theology lies firmly in the crux of practice and theory (often called praxis), our hope is not in just proposing new ideas, but rather new ideas that have legs. Public pastoral theology is something that is equally thought and done; it is a theological orientation lived in relationship. As such, we are examining the myths of communities in the hope of finding new ways of strengthening life-giving practices while tearing down other stories that seek to destroy it. The abuse of fear by politicians, preachers, and others has a detrimental effect on society as a whole; thus we need to begin thinking anew about how we should respond as faithful people. For public theology to work, it must create a new story that reinterprets and refutes the narratives offered by those who peddle fear. Throughout this book, I have proposed hope as both a concurrent emotional state and as an alternative to the narratives of fear we experience. As we move into this wider narrative setting, actively living a life of hope becomes even more important. The greatest example of an active hope is to be found in the ways we love one another. If we think of hope as having both possible and probable components, then the possible is found in our creative visions for the future, and the probable is seen in the loving actions we undertake in each moment.

In many of the communal narratives of fear, love seems to be the primary missing ingredient. In our search for a public theology of fear and hope, love can provide a grounding principle for reinterpreting these myths. The most obvious place to begin to develop our sense of what love is, is the love ethic. For those who haven't heard this term before, the love ethic is simply the command to love God, neighbor, and self. As an orienting paradigm, command, or principle, this is not without its issues. We have spent countless years trying to define our neighbors or what a love of God looks like. Given the contemporary emphasis on self-esteem, we could be accused of a little more love of self than necessary. At different times, we have ordered these loves according to their level of importance, often to the neglect of one category or another. When I refer to the love ethic, I am referring to a set of interconnected and interdependent loves. That is, love of God necessitates love of what God loves, namely all of God's creation. Furthermore, love of creation and all its homogeneous and heterogeneous parts points us back to a love of the one who has given such gifts. The love of neighbor and self reflects the love of God, and love of God is expressed through our love of self and neighbor.[7]

To hold these three loves in a relational tension gives us a novel story to ground our interpretations of personal and cultural narratives. The constant working out of the tension between these loves speaks to the dynamic processes of life and the need to explore our imaginations, empathy, and interconnectedness. Furthermore, by grounding ourselves on the love ethic, we are reminded of the relational structure of life and immanence of God. Relational love is not something we have to figure out on our own, as we have an example in Jesus' life and God's passionate relationship to all of creation. As process philosopher Robert Mesle remarks,

> God is good because God shares the experience of every creature—every pain, joy, hope, despair, failure, and triumph. God is not an *im*partial, *dis*interested observer of the world but the uniquely "*omni*-partial" and *totally*interested participant in every relationship there is. God knows what it is like to be you and me and "them" and the animals and plants we all eat. In the fullest sense possible, then, God is love: God is perfect relational power.[8]

Mesle expresses why a relational attitude toward the love ethic is so important. Namely, goodness is found in sharing experiences with others; love comes from being involved, not isolated, from being interested rather than independent. Love is found in empathically connecting to the experiences of life together. We see love in imagining the experience of those in our world, but also in the novel possibilities that come with every experience. Through our accessing novel and creative ideas, love and hope share the purpose of reconnecting us to the goodness of life.

When we seek to reorganize stories that manipulate our capacity for fear, we are essentially seeking a greater harmony between the creative possibilities of hope and the construction of our relationship to the world. Creativity, novelty, beauty, contrast, and harmony are all theological themes that play a part in the reorganization of fear-based narratives. One of the unique hallmarks of the stories of fear mongers is that they plant in our imaginations the possibility of harm by a real, but generally quite removed threat. They give us something to fear, but it is something we would rarely experience. Terrorism, crime, socialism, and loss of freedom are all small examples of stories that engender fearful responses. Yet, most of us in the United States will not directly experience a threat related to one of these categories. At best, they function as imagined threats that create discord in our lives and interrupt our ability to love and care for one another. To reorganize these mythic fears, we must reorganize our imaginations and orient ourselves toward a more empathic and interdependent existence.

Looking at the world through the five process categories above can help us begin to reframe the role of these imagined threats. By way of simplified definitions, creativity refers to the dynamic processes of the world. It ensures that there is always something new, always a next moment. Even when we cannot see change occurring, creativity is asserting itself in myriad ways through the freedom of our action and/or inaction. Creativity is the source of possibility, as it allows us to see beyond the limits we set for ourselves. Novelty expresses the qualities of possibility in each new moment. In new moments, there are multiple novel possibilities, some good, some bad, and others that fall on the spectrum in between. The possibility of novelty is the result of an open future, where freedom allows us to have some choice in the direction our lives will take.[9] What this means is that we have choices in how we will reflect on and react to stories perpetuated on culture by fear mongers.

This leaves us with beauty and harmony to briefly define. "In process thought, the lure of God [Initial Aims] within each human life is not only a lure to live. It is also a lure to live well; that is, to live with beauty—with harmony and intensity—relative to the situation at hand."[10] Just as we discussed about fear, there is more to the emotion for meaning-making creatures than mere survival. If this is a choice, and the best choice for a circumstance, then it can be something of great beauty. It can be the source of our living well. At the same time, when fear is manipulated and abused, when it pushes us to the fringes of knowing and caring for one another, it is a source of discord. Beauty presents a bit of a quandary to define succinctly, as beauty is often subjective. Beauty represents an ideal form of experience. According to Alfred North Whitehead, "Beauty is the internal conformation of the various items of experience with each other, for the production of maximum effectiveness."[11] Beauty is the source of constructive goodness, but its meaning is derived through internal confirmation. At the same time, beauty helps us recognize that there is discord, as the sources of what is beautiful for one may infringe upon the interpretation of beauty for another.

While discord can often lack a constructive side, there are times when it can serve the function of aiding us in transitioning through life. Discord can provide hope at times and terror at others. As I look at the way that fear is manipulated, I can see how someone might intend to increase safety. On the other hand, the use of fear to separate, isolate, narrow choices, and increase one's own power at the expense of others provides more terror than hope at the end of the day. Thus as we seek to transform these stories, finding what is beautiful to you about faith, the divine-human relationship, human relationality, and our experiences in life will be vital fuel for the imaginative fire.

The most beautiful experiences are often thought to be some combination of intensity, harmony, and contrast. We can often find beauty in the space between harmony and contrast. If harmony describes the moments in life when things come together to create something great, then contrast explores the higher meaning that is sometimes found in contradictory elements of life. Contrast can call us into a more complex unity of thought through our experience of disparate objects. Contrast sees beauty in an unsettling experience.

However, this same complexity can be achieved in harmonious experiences. These are the moments when congruent experiences, beliefs, ideas, emotions, and so on coalesce to form a great complexity of thought and open up a variety of choices for interpretation and action. As things flow together, something greater than the sum of its parts is realized. Beauty is often found when these harmonious experiences are so intense that we cannot help but experience something far beyond our own creation or abilities. In process theology, it is often said that God's intentions and lure is to a life of greater and greater beauty.

Creativity, novelty, beauty, contrast, and harmony are themes that call us to see the world differently. In each of these theological categories we find different points of contact with a God who seeks to increase the life-giving aspects of our experiences. In creativity we find the hope for multiple pathways through moments in our lives; in novelty we can see the possibility of interacting dynamically with the world. Harmony and contrast provide the lure into something greater; they give us the hope that there is more, that as co-creators we can be privy to something bigger than ourselves. All of this culminates in the hope for a greater intensity of experience, and a life of beauty. What this means going forward is that our previous love ethic may be more akin to a love aesthetic.

What Does God Ask of Us?

Just as with individuals, a public theology of fear depends on our ability to experience and engage in acts of hope. As such, we must be willing to use our theological and empathic imaginations in the communities where we reside. Our goal should be nothing less than establishing a community of hope as a contrast to these stories of fear. To do this, we must be available to the possibilities contained in an open future. When our choices are restricted by those who sell these stories of fear, our ability to experience creativity and engage in novel behavior is diminished. In a sense, these threat peddlers become a god we worship as we cling to their answers and solutions rather than listening in faith to the myriad of possibilities before us. As they narrow our choices, we must find the courage to have hope. Even while the contrast of their fear-based stories and the solutions they offer may seem beautiful, we must risk asking if this is what our faith in God requires of us. Do the stories they tell lift up the value of all of God's creation? Are their solutions built upon a foundation of love, hope, and faith? As we seek to respond to these reflective questions, we might find that we can do better. However, this would entail our proffering new stories of hope and love that add complexity to our communities and relationships. It would require us to speak of love and justice as hopeful realities that all should be able to claim.

These novel stories need to develop in protest and righteous anger to the narrow faith and possibilities we are being sold in fear-based narratives. Stories of love and hope broaden the possibilities for greater good of as many people as possible. They tell of a love aesthetic, of an intentional intensity that claims the beauty of our relationships to one another. We must be more than just an ally of hope, love, and beauty; we must claim our role as activists who live these stories as well.

As we operationalize these protests, I can think of no better example than the simple call from the sixth chapter of Micah. In verse eight we are told what goodness entails, namely to love kindness, walk humbly, and do justice. Each of these acts of love requires us to engage our theological, pastoral, and aesthetic imaginations. To be kind, humble, and just means exploring our empathic imaginations and reaching out to others. Moreover, all of these acts of faith demand a sense of justice, specifically a restorative justice that seeks reconciliation of broken relationships. In the end, our small and large acts of protest shape a world where "[a]ll are a part; all have room to move around; all are spinning the web; all suffer from its breakage; all reap its benefits; all celebrate its durability; all engage its repair."[12] In this image of the web, we see a public theology devoted to empathy, interdependence, and imagination. Together they form the basis for acts of kindness that welcome and repair; acts of justice that share and celebrate; and acts of humility that recognize the humanity in all.

1. Think about the stories you read on a daily or weekly basis. What emotions do they bring up for you?

2. What solutions do you see being offered by people who peddle stories of alarm and fear? What are they offering you in exchange for hearing them out?

3. Rather than fear being right or wrong, I think that it is more helpful to understand fear and hope in the public sphere as they relate to increases in beauty or discord. How does this understanding change your ideas about fear and/or hope?

4. How have you seen your choices in life narrowed by stories of fear? Do stories of hope open new avenues of thought for you? If not, what does?

5. How might you imagine responding to people who peddle stories of fear so that our sense of community and connectedness can be restored?

Notes

1. I think about things like the "war on Christmas," manufactured by preachers and politicians to rally people to a cause. This fear-based movement has engendered verbally violent responses from its adherents. Even the fact that they use a term like war in relationship to the coming of the "prince of peace" shows the lack of understanding about the very thing they seek to protect. I can think of no other reason for this juxtaposition than to inflame a community to act with hostility toward those who take another position. The rallying cry is for the faithful to stand and fight against a perceived slight. If we apply the trifocal lens of humility, justice, and kindness to this fear-based narrative, there is no light under which the argument for an imminent threat against Christian values stands as a valid and faithful position to undertake relative to the cultural paradigms in which we live.

2. Mark Konty, Blythe Duell, and Jeff Joireman, "Scared Selfish: A Culture of Fear's Values in the Age of Terrorism," *The American Sociologist* 35, no. 2 (Summer 2004): 94.

3. Ibid., 95–96

4. Ibid., 95.

5. Larry Graham, *Care of Persons, Care of Worlds: A Psychosystems Approach to Pastoral Care and Counseling* (Nashville: Abingdon, 1992), 13.

6. Larry Graham, "Pastoral Theology as Public Theology in Relation to the Clinic," *Journal of Pastoral Theology* 10 (2000): 11.

7. This does not do away with the idea that anytime we express a love for ourselves there is the chance that the good things we want for ourselves will compete with the things that may be good for another. However, keeping a healthy tension between these three primary loves can offer us a reflective moment that may mitigate the impact of some of the more extreme things we do to express love for ourselves and others.

8. Robert Mesle, *Process-Relational Philosophy: An Introduction to Alfred North Whitehead* (West Conshohocken, PA: Templeton Foundation, 2008), 86–87.

9. This freedom is often constrained by past decisions and systems of power that keep us from exercising the full possibility of certain choices. That does not mean that God stops offering them, it just makes them harder to choose or enact. Freedom stems from the idea that God's perfect knowledge is related all knowledge that is knowable, the future is mysterious and therefore, open.

10. Jay McDaniel, "A Process Approach to Ecology," in *Handbook of Process Theology*, ed. Jay McDaniel and Daniel Bowman (St. Louis: Chalice, 2006), 238.

11. Alfred North Whitehead, *Adventures of Ideas* (New York: Free Press, 1967), 265.

12. Larry Graham, *Care of Persons, Care of Worlds*, 14.

9

Perfect Love Drives Out Fear

Rather than denigrating the fear we experience, even those fears raised through manipulative means, we must find a way to transform the passions fear creates. The simple response to the manipulative ways that preachers, teachers, and politicians use fear to galvanize a community around their (often) personal projects is to react hopefully with acts of love; it is to seek and share the beauty found in the contrasting or harmonious experiences of our lives. Rather than responses of violence, isolation, and even passive acceptance, we should feel called to respond with a relational love that stands in opposition to this heavy-handed rhetoric. A love like this seeks to engage rather than isolate; it looks for opportunities for justice, through being resilient in the face of a message of fear and resistant to the calls for violent action and rhetoric; it seeks to be humble, and to reflect a care for all of God's creation rather than an arrogant assumption that one choice fits all situations; it seeks to be a kind presence, finding a way to respect, out of a sense of God's enduring presence, all those whom God cares for and loves (which means everyone, for those who are wondering).

A love that drives out the fear dumped on communities must be relational, just as fear is relational. Love means little without relationship; furthermore, its impact is muted if it is only held out to communities that are homogeneous. Love means little if it is only offered to the people and communities we know will receive it; there is little risk in loving people who we know will return the favor. While loving those who would love us back may increase the beauty of that relationship, it does not bear the same intensity of experience as a love that requires us to take some risks. The kindness, humility, and justice of a love that drives out fear cannot merely be reserved for those we are closest to; our interconnectedness demands more. Love that drives out fear provides a contrast that creates complexity in our experiences. A relational love will actively resist the rhetoric that seeks to define and divide on the basis of fear. It stares down those who seek to manipulate us through messages of fear, and through kindness and humility negates these messages of hate, derision, and division. A love like this takes in these messages of manipulation and resists them through transformative acts of justice and a resilient hope based on the enduring knowledge of an intimate and active God.

Responding in love to abusive uses of fear is risky behavior; it requires us to participate in a dynamic and changing world; it sometimes means facing down discordant contrasts with little more than hope and possibility at our side. We must become reflective actors who engage those who would perpetuate fearful myths. A smile and a nod is not the type of kindness and humility that drives out fear. A passive stance toward the perpetuation of these well-spun myths does nothing more than confirm the messages of a purveyor of fear. A relational love acted out of kindness, humility, and justice is meant to transform.

In the case of these grand narratives of shared fear, kindness is more than being nice, humility challenges others in love, and justice seeks reconciliation through the restoration of relationships. A faith built on relational love must be willing to ask difficult questions of those who perpetuate myths of fear; if we cannot stand together on the side of love and hope in the face of an abusive use of fear, then we risk impotence. The first act of protest we can undertake is to reflect on fearful stories and their narrators through a lens of faith, love, and beauty. Does the person sharing this story seek to increase the love, kindness, and justice of the world? Do they speak from a place of humility? How are they using their positions of power to remind us of our interdependence? How are they appealing to our imaginations in ways that provide more harmonious choices that fit a faith grounded in love? Before we begin to protest, we must know what (and sometimes who) it is we are protesting. We don't protest out of a sense of rightness or a claim to a great truth. Our protest stems from the sense that God calls us into greater relationship with one another, and these divisive stories threaten that call. Our protest is against the discord caused by those who seek power through fear.

Before we begin talking about these three acts of faith, I want to add a caveat. While there is some overlap between the redemption of fear as an emotion and this public theological idea, there are some noted differences as well. As I talk about these three acts of love and faith, I see them as ways of transforming the energy and passion created by publicly manipulated stories that engender the emotion of fear. As responses and protests to certain themes that undergird fear-based myths, I think these virtues allow us to see different ways of interacting faithfully in a world of God's creation.

KINDNESS, HUMILITY, JUSTICE

As we explore each of these acts of protest to fear-based manipulations, I have paired them with common cultural myths that often have fear-based roots. I contend that these myths are in dire need of transformation if we are to experience the increasing harmony of faith and life that God seems to intend for us. I surmise that the hyper-individualism experienced in American culture can be traced to a fear of dependence. I believe this myth can be reorganized through acts of kindness. With humility, I examine the cultural myth of exceptionalism and its concurrent fear of being ordinary. Finally, I look at justice as the act that can transform stories that paint difference as something to fear. My sense is that these stories hide a fear of being wrong.

KINDNESS AND A FEAR OF DEPENDENCE

In an article titled "Religion as Culture," psychologists Adam Cohen and Peter Hill say the following:

> American culture is highly individualistic relative to other countries. . . . Influences on American individualism have been theorized to include, for example, the political philosophies of the American founding fathers, the emphasis on individual rights and freedom, limited government, the American market economy, and American frontier life.[1]

One of the great myths of our culture centers on the themes of independence and individualism. We are taught early on that rugged individualism is a preferred lifestyle. Americans are to brave new territory alone, facing the world and shaking our fists at the ways it tries to hold us back. Children are schooled in the ideas that success or failure is often the result of our own work. We idolize entrepreneurs and disparage welfare recipients; we deify those we believe pulled themselves up by their own bootstraps. As a culture, we seem to look down on those who admit needing help as weak. We blame the victim, calling them lazy, unstable, or irresponsible. We take our individualism so seriously that we sometimes place individual rights and opinions above the common good. Today, an argument can be made that anything that is seen as good for the whole is often equated with socialism or infringing on our rights as individuals. We laud political positions and laws that champion the rights of individuals; by the same token, laws meant to be good for the whole nation are derided as creating a welfare state, socialism, or breeding dependence. People who sacrifice for the common good or compromise to the get the best result are seen as weak and lacking personal conviction; unless, that is, we can make individual heroes out of them, make them worthy of worship. The values of independence and individualism have worked their way into a love for self that is little more than a thinly veiled selfishness.

This emphasis on individualism has crept into the church as well. Some of most popular Christian understandings of salvation and faith boil them down to an individual choice. John Suk, in a *Christian Century* article, says this:

> The bottom line is that the huge emphasis that contemporary evangelicals put on a great personal experience of and with Jesus has little or nothing to do with scripture and everything to do with taking from our culture what it thinks human happiness is all about.[2]

In a quest for happiness, we seek out individual ways of attaining some satisfaction.[3] Thinking about faith as solely a personal decision or solo relationship with God goes against the grain of scripture and thousands of years of church tradition. The whole idea that I make a choice to believe in God, or that I choose to be "saved" or "born again" is a slap in the face to a benevolent God. Our language is of a personal relationship with Jesus; we say we are spiritual but not religious, that we don't need communities of faith in order to have faith. It's my faith, my time, my way, so butt out. We have to make it personal before communal. As though the decision to be loved by God was something we had a choice of in the first place.

I think our vehement defense of independence and individualism hides a more pervasive theme. Namely, we are afraid of being dependent. If you look at our culture, we are fed a constant stream of stories and opinions that denigrate ideas of dependence. We look down upon people who are dependent, afraid that we might become them. We pity the elderly whose bodies or minds may have failed them, and hide them from our sight; we generalize about the weakness of the sick, the poor, and the oppressed. The first lesson our children learn (mine included) is that it's important to be independent, and independence breeds confidence. All of this banter and bluster hides our fear of being dependent upon someone or something else. I think this fear has hardened us; it has tarnished our ability to be empathic; it has allowed us to buy in to the vitriol and hate that fear mongers feed us, complete with their readymade assumptions and solutions. In our quest to rise to the top, we forget the kindness of others who helped us get there.

My sense is that our fear of dependence is derived through cultural stories that uphold independence and individualism as primary tenets for living in the

United States. Thus we have created economic categories to determine whether or not someone measures up to our ingrained cultural values: rich, poor, job-creator, welfare queen, independent, co-dependent, or dependent. A simplified example of the pervasiveness of these categories is that the person who helps me with my taxes sent us a card at the birth of our second daughter, which basically congratulated us on her arrival and alerting us to the fact that we now receive a second tax deduction.[4] Of course this is a lighthearted and laughable example, but one with a much deeper meaning. We like to play zero-sum games with humans, weighing their performance against an economic standard to determine their worth. Even our churches employ the language of "giving units," imposing an economic sensibility onto communities of faith. In doing this, we lose. We lose sight of another's humanity; we lose perspective on any idea of a creative goodness we carry with us; and in turn, we lose the ability to empathically connect in interdependent ways.

Regardless of our perspective on faith, rampant individualism and independence is almost inexcusable. Our protest against stories of fear begins by pointing out the contrast between this cultural narrative of independence and the dependence upon God we are meant to experience. Simply put, we are dependents; dependent upon grace; dependent upon faith; dependent upon God's love; dependent upon one another. We are dependent on the kindness of a God who remembers us. We are dependent on the kindness of people who help us reach our goals, who protect us from danger, who challenge us to grow and dream. We are dependent on our ability to be kind to ourselves, not overlooking failure but rather transforming it through our responsibility to God, neighbor, and self. Communities are interdependent, or they aren't communities at all. In gratitude for the interdependent lives we lead every day, our faith calls us into a kindness for one another that stems from the simple belief that as we are all human, we all deserve the respect that humanity bestows upon us. In this way, kindness is about justice, it is about accountability, and it is about responsibility. Our protest begins with these narratives that reframe dependence and provide a contrast to our culture. Yet, our words are never enough.

Kindness is a call of faith, and flows from our ability to cultivate an empathic life. A kind faith will challenge and console, connect and care. It has little to do with liking or approving of every person and their actions. Rather it is about extending hospitality to ourselves and others. Kindness remembers that we do not walk in this world alone; that our lives are built in relationship rather than an isolated independence. In being kind to one another, "we acknowledge that every one of us shares the same wish to be happy, and often a similar confusion as to how to achieve that happiness. We also recognize that we share the same vulnerability to change and suffering, which elicits a sense of caring."[5]

Coming out of one perspective on the Jewish tradition, kindness is thought to be one of the cardinal virtues of the community, and it can be seen in a variety of ways. In a study of Ruth, Russell Hendel describes four important and distinct forms of kindness. Verbal kindness is expressed not just in greeting someone, but with the inclusion of a blessing; social kindness is seen in the provision of food, clothing, shelter, loving relationships, and restoration of one's lifestyle after hardship; vocational kindness stems from creating a work environment that allows others to achieve their goals in a dignified work environment; and finally, reputational kindness seeks to protect another's reputation and increase their standing in society.[6] As you can see, kindness is more than being nice. It is an all-encompassing metaphor for a relational justice that seeks to highlight our responsibility to treat one another with the kind of respect that our common humanity accords in all facets of life. Moreover, these types of kindness have the power to transform fears of dependence through meaningful relationships that call us into a greater awareness of our interdependence.

In order to be kind, we must attend to our empathic imaginations. We have to be able to visualize the humanity in everyone around us. We have to look beyond labels that economize, categorize, and stigmatize human beings. In an earlier chapter, I described empathy as the ability to experience and express what someone else is going through. It is through empathy that we gain a window into what it means to live through the eyes of another; it is through kindness that we seek to aid in their continued growth and understanding of the world. Kindness is not about imposing our views of the world on someone else, but making sure that everyone has the proper ingredients of life to succeed. Kindness makes the world more complex, opening the door to greater possibility and choice. Kindness is less about charity, and more about taking a passionate stance toward developing interdependent life. Kindness empowers others, enabling them to claim their humanity where some might wish to steal it. We cannot underestimate the power kindness has to drive out a fear of dependence. A fear of dependence stems from a fear of being taken advantage of by another. Kindness drives out this feeling through a genuine concern for the well-being of others. Kindness expresses the very simple notion that we are all connected to one another. Moreover, that connection reveals our responsibility to one another.

Stories that fuel the flames of independence and in turn our fears of being dependent simply lead us into a greater isolation from one another. As with crime, the more we hear we need to protect ourselves, the less we relate to one another. We isolate, we run from a fear in order to survive. In turn, we lose the capability to thrive through the power of a relational love and kindness. Interdependence is as inescapable as fear. To describe a community as interdependent is to see it as an empowered group of people who support one another, while at the same time giving room for individuals to live their own stories. An interdependent community thrives on the value of kindness to stave off fears that would harm the one or the many. Furthermore, an empathic kindness invigorates a sense of the holy in the other. It reminds us that we are not alone in bearing an image of God, but that this burden and joy is shared by all of humanity.

HUMILITY AND A FEAR OF BEING ORDINARY

Roughly halfway through my college career I came home on a break, full of the knowledge that college instills. Wanting to share with my folks that they had not completely wasted their money (there is that economization of humanity again), I decided to dazzle them with my newfound critical-thinking skills. While sitting at a meal with my parents, I asked, "What is the greatest lie that parents tell their children?" My dad, in a "this should be good" kind of voice, replied, "Enlighten us." I responded that the greatest lie parents tell their children is, "You can be anything you want to be when you grow up." To this day, I believe this is the only thing I have ever told my dad that he still repeats to others.

From an early age, many children are indoctrinated into a dominant American myth around exceptionalism. Average is for people who don't apply themselves, who don't work hard enough. We are to do something with our lives, be something great, and achieve success beyond our wildest dreams. We are told by doting parents as we close our eyes to dream, that we can be anything; that there are no limits to what we can achieve. I find this myth troubling in a number of ways, not the least of which is the creation of a sinister have-and-have-not mentality.

Part of the fuel that I think feeds this cultural myth is our long history of American exceptionalism. As Stephen Walt suggests,

> Most statements of "American exceptionalism" presume that America's values, political system, and history are unique and worthy of universal admiration. They also imply that the United States is both destined and entitled to play a distinct and positive role on the world stage.[7]

It should be noted that exceptionalism is nothing new or even unique to the United States. Countries throughout the ages have engaged in the kind of jingoistic chest-thumping that Americans have been doing for the last two hundred years. Everyone wants to believe that somehow they are special, that their brand of politics, religion, lifestyle, family dynamics, children, and/or culture is better than those around them; alternatively, if they do not measure up to the cultural myth, narratives of failure and exclusion can dominate the landscape of a life.

In response to the American athletes' performance at the 2012 London Olympics, commentators on Fox News complained about their lack of patriotism and jingoistic zeal. Their uniforms didn't reflect the nation's colors; they didn't wrap themselves in the flag enough, or spend enough time on the podium talking about American superiority.[8] The narrative of American exceptionalism is forced upon the world with a kind of religious fervor and flavor, instantly setting up an us-versus-them mentality.

This approach to life, the world, and our place in it has some deleterious effects. When exceptionalism becomes a belief, it becomes harder to open ourselves to criticism, especially when that criticism is warranted. Pastoral theologian Ryan LaMothe describes it this way:

> Whether secular or religious, exceptionalism is inherently problematic because those who are not chosen, those who are not in my exceptional group, are, more often than not, constructed as something less than full persons. Of course, there are instances when the stranger is welcomed, but by and large, individuals and nations who see themselves as exceptional tend to act in ways toward the Other that exhibit less than mutual-personal associations. U.S. exceptionalism, when combined with capitalism and militarism, makes for a heady brew of nationalistic pride that often results in constructing non-U.S. people as inferior. At best, the inferior peoples are pitied and, at worse, they become objects to be exploited, evangelized, or destroyed.[9]

Exceptionalism has a way of breeding feelings of superiority that lack a basis in reality. There is nothing kind about exceptionalism when it becomes an unquestioned belief. We can be great, without having to be the greatest; we can be exceptional, without having to proclaim ourselves as the exception. Ultimately, exceptionalism reveals a lack of mutuality; it separates and categorizes; it turns the other into something to be derided for their lack of status, rather than empathizing with others based on our common humanity.

It is fascinating how this belief has inserted itself into religious and theological circles. We used to measure exceptional churches by their membership numbers; today, exceptional churches are measured by the depth of their spirituality or their service-mindedness. We set up arbitrary categories that compare people, organizations, and nations in order to claim or recognize superiority. Exceptional ministers are expected to rise to the top of large congregations. Everyone wants the best preachers and teachers to head their organizations because that means they have some claim to superiority over other churches in their area. Even in our interpretations of Jesus' ministry, we qualify the crowds he draws as counting only men. I understand the inclusive bent of doing this, but there is also something more satisfying and exceptional in saying that Jesus preached to or fed 10,000 rather than 5,000. We actively look for ways to make things exceptional, often at the expense of making them simply better.

This insidious exceptionalism exacts a heavy toll on us as individuals and communities. Children are placed under greater and greater pressure to perform academically and athletically. Adults measure their superiority through material, familial, or personal success. It is hard to develop community when we are attuned to finding faults in others in order to gain an advantage. Not only are we unable to accept critique, but we also lose perspective on failure. We come to believe that an exceptional nation, teacher, preacher, spouse, child, self, or friend cannot fail. Our pride in our exceptionalism means that failure is not an option, and we are unsure what to do when the inevitable happens.

One of the greatest fears that failure reveals is that we are ordinary, and few people want to believe they are ordinary. Christians of all walks have spent years cultivating the idea that as children of God we are exceptional! When we read the parable of the talents, we are the people who received the ten talents, while "others" received the five talents or one. There is no room in our world for being the recipient of a single talent. There is no pride in receiving the least amount of prestige in the group. Pride, whether a nationalistic zeal, an incomplete examination of one's own talents, or just an outrageous expectation of exceptionalism, is not often held up as a Christian virtue. Yet, our faith in our exceptionalism is a political, religious, and cultural reality. Our kids are smarter than your kids; our nation is greater than your nation; I am better than you. For a person or an entity to be exceptional, a contrast must be established; someone or some entity must be ordinary or average; for me to be beautiful, you must be ugly. There is a great insecurity in this faith in exceptionalism. Our fear here is that we are the contrast to the extraordinary people. Therefore, we rush to label others as inferior before they can find out just how ordinary we truly are.

Truth be told, there is nothing wrong with being ordinary, as long as we remember we are unique. There is nothing wrong with telling our children that they have a unique gift or a plurality of talents that will enable them to do a lot of things in life. There is nothing wrong with being good enough. Ultimately though, what will drive out and transform this fear of being ordinary, and its symptom of exceptionalism, is humility. Humility can provide a healthy dose of realism that challenges the entitlement and otherness of exceptionalism. It also invites those who have been deemed unexceptional to the table. To walk humbly in this world is not to be a doormat or a pushover. To be humble requires inner strength and confidence; it takes someone capable of seeing what is happening around them and acting interdependently.

In Elizabeth Hinson-Hasty's words, to be humble is to engage in a process of

> deheroizing ourselves as individuals, recognizing the value of ordinary activities, and seeing how transformation occurs as we live in connection with a broader community. In genuine humility, she recognizes that she is not called to individual fortune, fame, recognition, and accomplishment as an "I," but that her call is part of a larger "we."[10]

Heroes have always been important in the dominant American culture, whether it occurs when we look in the mirror, at our children, or at people in powerful places. Humility breeds the kind of confidence that helps us see our place in a local community. It allows us to understand the impact of our words and actions, seeing that whether I succeed or fail, there is more to the process than just me. Humility challenges the dichotomy of exceptionalism by helping us realize that all have value, all have a voice, and all are uniquely talented.

Psychologists who have studied the phenomenon of humility describe it as

> an accurate sense of one's abilities; the ability to acknowledge mistakes, imperfections, gaps in knowledge, and limitations; openness to new ideas, contradictory information, and advice; keeping one's abilities and accomplishments in perspective; low self-focus or an ability to "forget" the self; and an appreciation of the value of all things.[11]

While this description may suit most research definitions, we have to be careful that it takes into account the experiences of oppressed populations. Humility doesn't go out looking for the poor, oppressed, or broken, but calls us to see ourselves in those same categories. It doesn't run out and help; it empowers people, through the knowledge of our own limits and failures, to relate to their experiences differently. Like kindness, humility requires a great deal of empathic imagination. Humility connects with the experience of others, and by taking away the entitled hero, seeks to bring them back to a community that cares. As Hinson-Hasty remarks, "the humility that grows out of service beyond the self challenges our society's expectation that we as human beings must make heroes out of ourselves."[12]

When we can look in the mirror and accurately gauge our talents and abilities; when we can acknowledge corporate and individual mistakes and limitations; when criticism can be seen with a constructive eye toward being a better person or community; and when we can celebrate appropriately our successes without worshiping them, then there is a chance that humility might begin to take root. The moment we face the reality of our gifts and talents, and see their place in the broader community, is the moment our protest begins. For this kind of humility to transform the cultural myths of exceptionalism and the concurrent fear of being ordinary, it

> must always be understood as a means of seeing oneself as part of the larger, interdependent earth, in relationship with the larger community, and as an integral part of transforming attitudes, structures, organizations, and institutions that marginalize people who differ from the dominant norms.[13]

Humility requires us to be strong enough to risk failure; it requires the courage to reach out to others with a genuine hope of empowering them.

A genuine humility becomes transformative when it connects people to one another through the measure of talents and gifts each one has. It doesn't look for heroes, or worship the exceptional. Humility sees the exceptional possibilities in everyone and seeks to cultivate the kind of community where those possibilities have a chance to shine in their own time and space. It's not that the ordinary suddenly becomes extraordinary, but rather that people become unique in their own right. The greatest casualty may be the cliché that children can be anything they want to be when they grow up; however, in its place comes the idea that every child can be something, and this something directly reflects their unique talents and creativity. Ultimately, it would seem that humility signals a greater self-confidence whereas exceptionalism merely shows a brash immaturity.

JUSTICE AND A FEAR OF BEING WRONG

The refrain shouted from pulpits and press conferences is that America is a Christian nation. Talking heads expound upon their version of history, exhorting us to remember that this nation was founded upon Judeo-Christian beliefs, morals, values, and ethics. They point to minor moments in times past to build a revisionist history and to railroad anyone who might think differently. As the rhetoric grows louder and louder, it becomes clear that differences will not be tolerated. Those who do not share these views of American history are labeled godless secularists, untrustworthy, and often at best deviants. As Christians become a focus group for politicians to pander to, believing in this revisionist history becomes tantamount to a religious test in order to hold public office (something, by the way, the Constitution strictly prohibits; see article 6, clause 3). But it has a more insidious effect of creating insider/outsider categories related to who deserves just treatment under the law. Christian activism in the political realm is in need of grand transformation if we are to truly live out the values we purport to espouse.

Instead of promoting a more just society, the recent past suggests that the entanglement between the church and state has created a myth that difference is intolerable. The narrative of a Christian nation has created a type of religious exceptionalism that pits religions against one another in order to develop and maintain superiority. There is nothing wrong with stating what is uniquely Christian; the difficulty we face is that the public Christianity[14] of today is more concerned with power, status, and the rightness of the order of things. Theologian Nicholas Wolterstorff puts it this way:

> With sorrow I must concede that a good many of my fellow Christians have failed us here in recent years. They have not seen it as their responsibility to present in the public arena their views on justice for all and the common good. Instead they have seized and manipulated the levers of power to secure and advance freedom for religious people and to inscribe their views on social issues into law, regardless of the views of others on the same issues.[15]

This is in stark contrast to ideas of humility, kindness, and justice that we find in the biblical tradition as well as Christian and Judaic historical narratives.

The search for power and the demand that a single narrative govern the entire society is antithetical to the command to do justice. Many of the powerful voices of public Christianity are little more than bullies who attempt to rule by fear and intimidation. Whether referring to a different theological stance, a different religion, a different culture, economic status, race, gender, or sexuality, the narratives of fear seem to center on the idea that accepting difference is a life-or-death decision. This myth that difference is harmful spreads through the rhetoric and stories of the culture, creating division, distrust, and in some cases death.

To be different today means risking being bullied and belittled by a ruling elite who seek to impose a level of conformity that is impossible to obtain in a globalized society and world. There is little kindness in these extreme positions and a severe lack of humility among the loudest proponents of these ideas. However, what may be missing most is the kind of justice that drives out the fear poured into the public sphere by those whose hatred of difference is driven by their fears. Moreover, when coupled with a penchant for American exceptionalism and the superiority/inferiority complex that accompanies it, being different can be downright dangerous today. While there is an overt fear of difference that runs through these stories, there also seems to be a fear of being wrong that pervades our rhetoric. So much so, that we would rather double down on a lie we believe, than hear about the facts that may drive us to a different conclusion. Our intolerance of difference, our fear of being wrong, reinforces our suspicion of the other and makes any attempt at doing justice difficult at best.

Respect for an alternative story does not have to negate the veracity of our own stories. It may challenge certain assumptions or beliefs related to an idea we have or an event we experience. There are numerous options we have when encountering a new story, idea, or belief. However, given the fear with which we approach difference, the myopia it engenders seems to enable us to respond in only a few ways. The first is that we tend to see an alternative story as destructive and thus defend our own point of view against all other claims. Another way we approach difference is to discount the storyteller and devalue their perspective or personhood until their version is discredited. Out of a fear of being wrong, we attempt to assert or legislate our opinions, beliefs, or ideas before another idea has time to take root. If that doesn't work, we just yell. We state our opinions or beliefs over and over again, even if it is proven false, until it becomes the dominant story. We believe that if something is said loudly and forcefully enough, especially if it garners media attention, then it must be true. As a result, ignorance and intolerance become cultural values that perpetuate fears of difference. Furthermore, the complete lack of humility often displayed by media-created heroes ensures that we are unable to admit when we are wrong as well as when our ideas are failures. Rather than admit being wrong, people claim they misspoke or were misquoted or that they have an offbeat sense of humor. We seem to be immune to the real impact our words have on the stories created and perpetuated by a populace that refuses to reflect on the myths they are handed.

The cry for restorative justice will be in stark contrast to these powerful narratives. Orienting ourselves toward doing justice means embracing difference. It means realizing the advantages we have received as part of a dominant subculture. "Justice cannot be founded on simply treating everybody the same as not everyone has equal standing to begin with."[16] Justice makes things more complex, rather than simplifying our stories. It does not seek to impose the views of a dominant subculture; rather it is humble enough to see how these views are contextually situated. We carry our histories with us wherever we go. Included in that are the advantages we receive from our ethnicity, gender, religion, sexuality, and economic status. These stories inform and inflame our beliefs, and as true as they are for us, they are not capital-T true for everyone. Our stories are but one drop in an ocean of narratives that are told and lived every day.

The cries of protest against a culture that demands homogeneity can only come from people seeking restorative justice. Generally speaking, there are three forms of justice that are discussed on a theoretical level. Retributive justice—which is the most popular idea about justice in the United States, even among Christians—seeks punishment for wrongs committed by an offender. Retributive justice, as stated before, is the type of justice often sought by people who see and experience the world fearfully. Distributive justice seeks the equitable distribution of goods among all people. Restorative justice is enjoying a surge among advocates for prison reform. Broadly speaking, restorative justice "offers a relational response to wrongdoing, focusing on the relationships that have been harmed and what needs to be done to repair those relationships."[17] More than kindness and humility, restorative justice protests stories of fear that paint difference as dangerous; however, it does so not with the intent of punishing an individual for perpetuating these narratives. Instead, its protest is in creating a transformative relationship with an offending party.

Those seeking restorative justice speak loudly of the contrast between stories that teach us to fear difference, and the radical inclusiveness of Jesus' ministry. However, the call we experience is not to speak justice, but to do justice. Justice is an act; it is a story we tell with the movement of our lives.

We will truly protest these manipulative stories of fear when we can get the offenders and offended in the same room to discuss differences and listen to one another. We must be advocates for the humanity of all, if there is to be an opportunity for justice to prevail. The lion must sit with the lamb, without the fear of there being a slaughter.

Coupled with kindness and humility, restorative justice makes hope both possible and probable. It is through restorative justice that the possibilities of reconciliation can be realized. Restorative justice requires deliberation rather than retribution. It requires us to relate rather than isolate. In the moments when a relationship of mutuality, humility, kindness, and concern are established, there is the possibility that grace can be realized through the complexity of difference. This requires a transformation of the arrogance that stems from a belief that our way is the only and right way. This is almost impossible without a resurgence of the kind of radical hospitality that welcomes the strange and stranger in our midst. It requires us to no longer deify dogma, and instead humble ourselves through the mystery of complexity. It is in these situations where we sit down with what is different and strange to us that the beauty of contrast can enrich our own beliefs while allowing for others to maintain their own ideas about what is good and right. In these moments, beauty replaces truth as the ultimate goal of a relationship. We will seek to increase the beauty experienced by all rather than increase the probability of rightness at the expense of another's supposed wrongness.

A RETURN TO CALVARY CHURCH

Calvary does one thing really well; it cares for its members and their families. When you look out at the congregation, you see a great deal of empathy that runs counter to the fears that many express. While these fears may dominate the discussions, there is a thread of hope ready to be explored in this caring orientation to one another. Therefore, you propose something to the leadership of the church.

You tell them that you have heard their fears, and that these are very real threats to their existence. You have heard how tired they are, how their legacy is in danger, how the people around them don't understand or want to relate to them. At the same time, you see how they care for one another, how they pour their hearts into the dwindling community and treat one another with respect and empathy. Where, you ask, does this energy come from? How do they muster the hospitality and compassion they share in this closed community? In short, you ask them to reflect on something they are doing that the larger world needs more of at this time. You point out the gentle and subversive protest that their community continues to take part in every time they relate to one another with kindness and humility. Ultimately, you pose a couple of questions for them to reflect upon. How might the community around them begin to experience some of this hospitality, compassion, and kindness? Furthermore, what is one simple thing they could imagine doing to reach out and express their desire to connect?

Together, these questions offer opportunities to expand their choices relative to their future as a community of faith, within a larger community. It takes their unspoken protests and makes it possible for them to become public and communal. They already have the energy to care for one another, and they do it well. What would it be like to expand this so that others could experience it? Rather than seeing others as different and unaccepting, it assumes that everyone is in need of relational contact, that everyone desires connection. Moreover, rather than the contrast they are creating with their stories of fear-producing discord, there is the possibility of a greater sense of beauty becoming part of the story.

Ultimately, this is how hope is reintroduced to the community, by reminding them that their story is still being written. Before them lie a myriad of choices, and through their empathy, imagination, and interdependence they can create stories of hope and love, of kindness and humility, that breathe a life of justice and reconciliation into the community around them. They have the opportunity to transform the passion and energy their fears create into possibilities for a new future. Their choices are not limited to life or death as a community of faith; they have the choice as to how they live and die; more importantly, they have a choice in the stories that will be told long after they are gone. These can be stories of isolation and fear, or they can be stories that remind people of what it means to love kindness, to walk humbly, and to do justice. The road ahead is not easy, you might remind them. However, the future is unwritten and the choice is theirs as to how they will be known by those who come next.

QUESTIONS FOR REFLECTION

1. Think about your relationships and communities. How do the people in these communities passively accept certain cultural fears? Name some ways you believe they also actively protest these same narratives.
2. How do the narratives of individualism, exceptionalism, and intolerance creep into your lives?

3. As you think about a fear of dependence, ordinariness, or wrongness, which of these is most present in your interpretation of the world?

4. Of kindness, humility, and justice, which do you believe is the easiest and/or hardest to employ in your life? What makes that virtue hard or easy for you?

5. What other values or virtues would you claim as helpful in transforming or protesting narratives of fear in our culture?

Notes

1. Adam Cohen and Peter Hill, "Religion as Culture: Religious Individualism and Collectivism Among American Catholics, Jews, and Protestants," *Journal of Personality* 75, no. 4 (2007): 710.

2. John Suk, "A Friend in Jesus? Faith Is Not a Personal Relationship," *Christian Century* 128, no. 18 (2011): 24.

3. As churches are subject to fewer and fewer loyalists, I don't think we can limit this kind of language to evangelicals alone.

4. My tax guy is a wonderful person who is much more complex than this simple statement. This example merely states how easily economic metaphors can creep into relationships and categorize or place value on a person.

5. Sharon Salzberg, "Mindfulness and Loving-Kindness," *Contemporary Buddhism* 12, no. 1 (2011): 178.

6. Russell Hendel, "Ruth: The Legal Code for the Laws of Kindness," *Jewish Bible Quarterly* 36, no. 4 (2008): 255–57.

7. Stephen Walt, "The Myth of American Exceptionalism," *Foreign Policy* 189 (2011): 72.

8. "Fox News Says Gabby Douglas' Leotard, Other US Olympic Uniforms Not Patriotic Enough," *The Huffington Post*, August 5, 2012, http://www.huffingtonpost.com/2012/08/05/gabby-douglas-us-olympic-uniforms-patriotism_n_1744172.html.

9. Ryan LaMothe, "A Pastoral Analysis of the Three Pillars of U.S. Hegemony—'Free Market' Capitalism, Militarism, and Exceptionalism," *Pastoral Psychology* 60 (2011): 191.

10. Elizabeth Hinson-Hasty, "Revisiting Feminist Discussions of Sin and Genuine Humility," *Journal of Feminist Studies in Religion* 28, no. 1 (2012): 112.

11. Julie Exline, "Humility and the Ability to Receive from Others," *Journal of Psychology and Christianity* 31, no. 1 (2012): 41.

12. Hinson-Hasty, 111.

13. Ibid., 112.

14. When I talk about public Christianity, I am referring to the "Christianity" of television, the media, and politics. There are certain places that the world turns when they need an inflammatory religious quote to sell their news. A politician's religious views are suddenly cast as the views of an entire faith or denomination. A television preacher who decides to burn a Koran or speak callously about the cause of a natural disaster suddenly represents large swaths of Christianity. There are many good faithful people, doing good things in the world, whose work never reaches the headlines. Often, the media crowns heroes of faith that the faithful would rarely choose themselves, and we become stuck with these images when a greater truth is known.

15. Nicholas Wolterstorff, "How Social Justice Got to Me and Why It Never Left," *Journal of the American Academy of Religion* 76, no. 3 (2008): 676–77.

16. Claudia Rozas, "The Possibility of Justice: The Work of Paulo Freire and Difference," *Studies in Philosophical Education* 26 (2007): 564.

17. William Pelech and Avery Calhoun, "Responding to Young People Responsible for Harm: A Comparative Study of Restorative and Conventional Approaches," *Contemporary Justice Review* 13, no. 3 (2010): 289.

10

Conclusion: Finding Hope

Finding hope in the stories that haunt us is no simple matter; it requires us to think about our experiences of the world in complex ways. To find hope in the moments that terrify us necessitates thinking about fear in new ways; this includes understanding the embodied nature of the emotion in our brains, and the embedded fears of our experiences. Moreover, it is important to remember that hope is not always about seeking something new, but about finding it in the cracks and fissures of experiences that trouble us.

Fear is a complex emotional state. It includes behavioral and physiological cues that remind us of its presence. When we are afraid, our field of vision narrows, we focus in on particular things in our environment; our muscles fill with blood as we prepare to respond; the blood drains from our faces and our digestive system shuts down to redirect energy to more vital systems. All of this stems from the activation of the amygdala, a well-connected bundle of neurons in our brains. This bundle of neurons responsively prepares us to react to something we feel threatens us; in addition, it is thought that the amygdala plays an important role in coding certain memories with the emotion of fear. When we encounter a threat, our bodies react, and we instinctually formulate a behavioral response. Fear most often engenders fight, flight, freeze, or appease responses. These behaviors, along with our embodied emotional response, can be thought of as revealing a desire to survive and cope with a threat or traumatic experience.

From an evolutionary perspective, fear has been conserved throughout our history. As a survival and coping mechanism, fear can be seen as an adaptive emotional state. It is intended to help us dynamically respond to novel experiences that threaten our existence. One of the most important things to realize from this embodied and evolutionary perspective is that fear is inescapable. It is not an emotion that we can turn off, ignore, or suppress without consequence. This information alone should give us pause to think theologically when we comment about fear in particular and emotions in general.

This theological pause in interpreting the emotion of fear (or emotions in general) stems from how we understand the *Imago Dei*. Simply put, the *Imago Dei* means "the image of God," and it has been described and defined in various ways since the early centuries of the Christian church. Using neurosciences to help define the *Imago Dei* requires us to think differently about our embodied selves. It requires us to incorporate novel findings about the brain into our sense of what it means to be human, and perhaps more importantly what it means to be human in relationship with God. When we begin to describe emotions as inescapable, it calls into question the primacy given to our rational lives. The neurosciences instantly make our theological interpretations of the divine-human relationship more complex. Accepting that emotions are integral parts of human experience necessitates thinking about God's emotional life as well. It requires us to take seriously God's passion for the world and humanity.

In traditional formulations of God, often the term *impassability* is used to describe God's dispassionate stance toward humanity and the world. With what we know of the embodied nature of emotions, I have proposed that a better way of thinking about God is through a lens of empath-ability. This means that God, at the very least, understands what it means to experience emotions, knowing their adaptive and meaningful qualities for humanity. A fuller understanding would be that God knows what it is like to be us, something we often subscribe to when we refer to the life of Jesus. For God to be empathic means that God experiences the suffering, joy, pain, anger, hurt, fear, happiness that humans know on a daily basis. It means that God's intimate immanence is shared with all of humanity and the world. If we can begin to think of God as empathically-able, then we can begin to think about emotions through theological lenses that value their impact on our lives. As a result, we can live into a faith that values the full range of human experience.

This exploration into the embodied nature of fear provides ample reason to explore what it means to be afraid. That is, if fear is adaptive, if it arises in the service of the continuation of life, if it is inescapable, then there may be more to understanding its role than just survival and coping with a sometimes hostile and unpredictable world. Fear may also serve some purpose in reconnecting us with what is life-giving. It may not only direct us away from a threat, but also direct us toward something we feel is worth living for. As a part of the divine-human relational matrix, fear can be God's best aim for a particular situation. Of the myriad choices we have, responding with fear may be a life-giving alternative to what we are facing. In this way, fear may be God's best hope in certain circumstances. Thinking about fear as an adaptive life-giving response allows us to think about the possibility of an undercurrent of hope that runs along with a fearful emotional experience. This complex way of interpreting the emotion of fear points to the inevitable cracks of resistance and resilience that are parts of just about every experience of a threat or trauma.

Through our experiences of fear and hope, we form memories and beliefs that shape the very core of our being. Emotional narratives shape and color our interpretations of the world; the more powerful the emotional experience, the more influence that experience may have on our lives. Emotional memories impact our beliefs about ourselves and the world around us, including our sense of what the future might hold. Yet, seeing fear and hope as concurrent emotional streams in our experience can help us reimagine our responses and open new interpretive possibilities. Ignoring or suppressing fear gives it more power than it deserves in shaping our reality. We need to see fear through its complex interrelationship with hope so that we might begin to understand how it can connect us to the goodness of life. We must begin to reshape our understanding of fear to reflect its complexity, and to reclaim its meaning for our faith and life.

I believe we must see that fear and hope are inextricably intertwined in our lives. Our desire for meaning is almost as inescapable as our experience of emotions. Fear is not just an emotion of survival and coping, but one that can point us toward a reconnection with the goodness of life; fear reveals the ways we seek to thrive in our environments. Undergirding our fearful reactions to threats and traumas is a current of hope, a connection to what is meaningful and beautiful that drives us to survive and cope. When we experience and respond in fear, we implicitly live out a reaction related to latent hopes for our lives. Fear and hope both occupy spaces in our minds that reveal connections to the present and future. In this way they also connect with our imaginations, giving rise to life-giving and life-limiting interpretations of the world. Thus our theological position must be that it is fine to be afraid; fear can be a natural and faithful response to certain situations we experience in life.

As we seek to counsel and care for those who have experienced threats and traumas in their lives, we must honor their fear. We should seek to empathize with rather than shame those who are afraid. Normalizing our experiences of fear can empower people to share their stories and seek the broader comfort by reconnecting them with a community that cares. Educating our communities of faith about the embodied and embedded nature of fear can help us reconnect with an immanent God who seeks relationship in all facets of our lives. Connecting our faith to our emotional lives can go a long way in reconnecting us with our embodied selves; it can remind us of our dynamic and adaptable qualities. Emotions feed our passions; they guide our steps and often remind us of what is important. We do ourselves and our communities a disservice when we willfully malign any emotional state and create a place where people feel ashamed to feel. An empathic community educated about our embodied emotions opens the doorway to encouragement for those who are experiencing inordinate amounts of fear. When we understand the complexity of fear and what it means, we can begin to see the fissures and cracks of hope in the fear-based stories we tell and hear. Having honored stories of trauma and the threats people experience, we can remind them of the ways they have resisted and faced these moments resiliently. We can stand with them in these moments of turmoil and respond authentically to the undercurrents of hope they may not be able to see themselves. We can empower them to see the "both/and" of their experiences—the ways they responded to a threat or trauma by surviving and coping, and the ways they implicitly acted with hope in order to reclaim the goodness of life by thriving in the face of a fear.

Equally important to these responses to individuals dealing with fear-based narratives is the way we can proactively respond to communal narratives that abuse the emotion of fear. As we explored, fear has been used by numerous sources to limit our choices and narrow our field of vision. Narratives that abuse the emotion of fear, causing us to separate ourselves from one another and seek the simplest response, dot the landscape of our lives. Through a variety of media sources, politicians, pundits, and preachers prey on our capacity to experience fear; the news shapes our discourse by dumping a variety of threats into our laps, creating a culture of fear. A proactive public theology of fear and hope requires us to develop responses to these narratives that shape our communities and relationships. Not only should we to empathize with, educate, and encourage people who experience threats and trauma, we should also be open to ways in which our faith calls us to respond to abusive uses of fear.

A proactive response to manipulative uses of fear seeks to transform their power and reconnect us to one another through humility, kindness, and justice. While I spoke about specific fears that these three qualities address, I believe they can be applied to a wider range of fear-based narratives that individuals and communities experience. The fears of being dependent, of being ordinary, of difference are far-reaching cultural narratives that impact our ability to connect with one another. Likewise, fears of crime, terrorists, and strangers affect our communal landscape. Approaching communal narratives of fear with an eye toward living out a transformative response can engender hope when times seem uncertain. When we respond to fear in our communities by sharing our faith, it would help to be a little humbler and kinder. When we act in response to tragedy and trauma, it behooves us to seek a restorative justice that brings about new and creative relationships.

The transformation of stories that haunt us begins with our relationships to one another. Fear is inevitable; it is natural; it is adaptive; it can even be the most hopeful of responses to certain experiences. We will be afraid; we must be afraid in order to survive and cope. However, we were never meant to live in fear. The latent hopes that give meaning to our fearful actions can give rise to a new interpretation of an experience. They can broaden our view of the world around us and enable us to reconnect to the goodness of life. To be afraid is to be a human being made in the image of God; of this we can be sure. However, fear does not have to be the last word in the stories of our lives. To understand fear in the context of faith is to remember the God who gifted us with this emotional life; moreover, it is to seek hope in the moments when our resolve falters. It is to remember the presence of God, dynamically and intimately intertwined with the life of the world; to be human and to be afraid is to realize that there is something hopeful worth living for. In this way, we can look at fear and not be afraid; instead, we can experience the presence of God that moves through all moments, calling us into a greater and greater hope.

Index